HOW TO MAKE SURE YOUR LIFE DOESN'T SUCK

A DIFFERENT KIND OF GUIDE TO NAVIGATING
THE UPS AND DOWNS OF LIFE

DR. MAGGIE GILEWICZ

Copyright © 2020 by Dr Maggie Gilewicz
All rights reserved.

No part of this book may be reproduced in any form or by any electronic or mechanical means, including information storage and retrieval systems, without written permission from the author, except for the use of brief quotations in a book review.

www.drmaggieg.com

FOREWORD

When I first met Maggie, I was impressed. She was a whirlwind of energy, pursuing her doctorate with a fierce desire to learn and an equally fierce commitment to being of service others. The only problem, as I came to see quite quickly, was that her life kind of sucked. Fortunately, as you will learn in this wonderful book, our experience of life can change in a single moment.

Let's face it - we all have shit going on in our lives from time to time. Our finances get out of control, the people we work for make ridiculous demands, the people closest to us let us down, and the whole world seems to have gone temporarily insane.

Perhaps worst of all, we feel like we are letting ourselves and others down with our inability to do what we know at our best is the best way forward. We get caught up in low moods and feel unable to break free. Our own thoughts and feelings turn dark, and the world around us seems to darken in response.

But no matter how hopeless and 'suckish' things may seem,

there is a quiet light waiting for us in the noise of the darkness. Our experience is not made up of our circumstances. We live in the feeling of what Maggie calls our THOUGHT-created realities, not the feeling of the outside world.

The American physicist David Bohm pointed to the nature of our personal realities when he wrote "THOUGHT creates our world and then says 'I didn't do it.'"

The Scottish mystic Syd Banks pointed to the same thing when he wrote "THOUGHT is not reality, yet it is through THOUGHT that our realities are created."

In my own work, I often liken this power of THOUGHT to play dough. Whether we use it to create animals or aliens, random shapes or barbershops filled with customers, the common element in each and every form is the raw clay from which it is made. And when we start to see that no matter how long we've been making the same shapes we can always start over and make something new, life gets considerably less scary and considerably more fun.

You won't find any exhortations in this book to "be more disciplined" or "cultivate a positive mental attitude". There are no techniques to practice and no practices you need to incorporate into what may already at times seem like an overly busy life.

This is because when you wake up to the fact of THOUGHT, you wake up to the infinite creative potential inside you. Whether you laugh with joy at the freedom you discover or cry with relief at the realization that you are (and always have been) OK, your life will never be the same again.

I was fortunate to be there the moment that Maggie had her

'aha' moment and woke up to her deeper nature – the power and possibility that is alive at the heart of all of us. And my fondest hope for you as you read this wonderful book is that you have an awakening of your own along the way.

In one of my early books, I wrote about it like this:

"Imagine you are dreaming the most incredibly vivid dream of your life", began the teacher. "In the dream, you seem to be some sort of adventurer, and each adventure brings with it new challenges and creative solutions. You experience many things – some wonderful and some not so wonderful.

You soon realize that in your dream, anything is possible. On one of your adventures, you encounter a very high wall, so you imagine yourself a rope and climb to the top. In another, you are falling off a cliff, but before you reach the ground, you begin to fly.

Eventually, you begin to look forward to each new adventure – until one time, for no apparent reason, everything seems to go wrong,

It is dark, so dark that you cannot see your hand before your face. Even before you can hear or see anything, you sense danger. Strange and uncomfortable sounds begin crawling out from the depths of your imagination and seem to be coming closer to you.

Cautiously, you strike a match. Everywhere you look, you're surrounded by the most hideous creatures you've ever seen.

You try to run, but your legs won't move; you open your mouth to scream, but no sound comes out. Everything you've learned up to this point seems to have abandoned you, and a horrific death seems imminent.

What would you do?"

The student was lost in thought for many moments, and the teacher could see a range of fearful emotions play across her face as she lived the scenario fully in her mind. Suddenly and without warning, she opened her eyes and began to laugh.

"I know what I would do," the student said. "I would wake up!"

Think of this book as a wake-up call from a dear friend. The life you change just might be your own…

With all my love,

Michael Neill

Author of *The Inside-Out Revolution* and *The Space Within*

Los Angeles, January 2020

"What can I tell you? All truth comes from within.

I cannot tell you anything you don't already know.

The search for truth is really the search for one's true self.

When people truly understand who they already are, they realize that they are part of the divine.

This understanding cannot come from the intellect alone or be simply given to you by others.

It must come from a place deep inside.

Know yourself, noble friend and you will know what you are searching for."

Michael Meade
Fate And Destiny: The Two Agreements Of The Soul

INTRODUCTION

The path to enlightenment with the gurus, spiritual promises, and self-help books are like a Big Mac.

Although it might feel good consuming it in the moment, it does not truly nourish us and, half an hour later, we are hungry again and looking for more.

Seph Fontane Pennock

I remember times in my life when I would reach out for self-help books whenever I felt low, anxious, insecure, or lost. I remember how I felt in those moments and how I was desperately looking for something, so I could change how I felt. And that's because, at the time, I was afraid of what I was feeling. I would freak out every time I felt depressed or anxious. What I also remember is, whenever I was experiencing those feelings, I thought there was something wrong with me, particularly when it seemed to me it was either happening too often, or it lasted far too long. And I believed something in my life—my work, my relationship, where I lived—had to change so I could feel better, or that something (a strategy, tool, practice, a self-help book, seminar) or someone (a coach, guru, therapist) could change how I felt.

I also remember that by the time I got to read a self-help book, I was so caught up in thinking—I was so invested in trying to change how I felt—that all I saw when I was reading it were words, but no meaning. Sometimes, I would find the content inspiring and, for a moment, I felt better and ready to use the tools or strategies I found in many of those books. But this feeling would never last and, sooner or later, I'd give up on the tools and on the strategies too. So, I'd look for another book. And every time I opened another and then another, I hoped that "that" book might finally turn out to be "the one" that would change my life. More importantly, it would help me change how I felt.

However, whatever I read and whatever advice I followed, sooner or later, I'd be back to feeling like crap again. Often, I'd feel worse because now I'd think of myself as a lost cause. How I felt still sucked, and because of it, my life sucked too.

I found myself in this loop a few times throughout my life. At the time, I thought I should not feel uncomfortable, anxious, or insecure; that I should never feel lost or stuck. So, I was constantly trying to change. Change how I felt or change myself. I was chasing after the elusive "positive state" or "happiness" because I thought it was possible for those states to be permanent. And a lot of self-help books and advice I came across innocently perpetuated the idea that I should feel good all the time, that I should be productive, or happy, or on top of the game, confident, in control, etc. most of the time. And if I didn't, it was a problem. So, I should find out what the problem was and try to solve it. At the very least, there was always something I should be better at, something I should fix or improve about myself, which meant that I was not OK or not enough the way I was. The search for tools, strategies, and practices continued because all the books I read seemed to convey the idea that I would have to forever rely on what they taught, as opposed to my own inner wisdom.

Thankfully, a few years ago, I experienced what some people describe as an "insight," an "aha' moment, an "awakening," or "epiphany." I saw my life and myself in a completely different way, and for the first time in my life, I experienced a sense of well-being like I never thought possible. All the problems I had before that moment happened were still there, but they no longer looked problematic. I understood, on a deeper level, how our experience of life is created, and how and why we feel one way or another about other people or our circumstances.

But what made the biggest difference to me was the realization that I did not have to be afraid of my thoughts. And, if I did not have to be afraid of my thoughts, I did not have to be afraid of my feelings and emotions. So, I stopped fighting my feelings, trying to get rid of them, and I stopped trying to change my thoughts.

For the first time, I felt a huge sense of relief, and I felt the freedom to be fully myself. Freedom to feel good and freedom to feel bad. Freedom to feel courageous and the freedom to be scared. Freedom to feel anxious and freedom to feel at peace. Freedom to be human. Ever since my epiphany, I have been able to be OK even when I don't feel OK, and, because of that, I have been able to experience well-being and enjoy my life much more and more often.

I wrote this book because I wish someone had told me much,

much earlier, what I now know: deep down, I have always been OK with all my thoughts and all my feelings. I may not have understood that straight away, but I would get curious enough to try to understand that and see it for myself. I wish that someone had told me that the more I try to change, manipulate, resist, or get rid of "bad" feelings, the longer they will persist.

I wish someone had told me that whenever I felt I was not enough or not OK, it was because I learned somewhere that I should be wiser, different, more positive, or more enlightened. That every time I wasn't feeling OK, it was not because there was something inherently wrong with me, but because my own wisdom and my natural OK-ness got lost not only in the ocean of other people's opinions, ideas, and concepts but also in the ocean of my own thoughts about who I should be, what I should be doing and how I should be doing it.

I wish someone had told me that I have always had everything already within me to deal with the ups and downs of life, and all I needed was someone to help me see that for myself. I wish someone had told me that my intuitive hunches, the "aha moments" and "gut feelings"—even though they cannot be measured or rationally explained—matter, and are an intrinsic part of my intelligence. I wish I had known that, before I set new goals and make choices, I should consult my inner self first before I consult or listen to anyone else, whether they are my friends, my parents, gurus or experts because only I know who I truly am and what I truly desire.

I wish I had known that nothing on the outside could change how I feel on the inside. That no amount of money, a better career, a nicer house, different circumstances, have anything to do with my contentment and well-being. Those things may bring a temporary sense of satisfaction, a bit of fun, and excitement, but none of those feelings will last because a true sense of happiness and well-being can only come from within.

I wish I had known that it is not life, people, or my circumstances that create my feelings but that my thoughts create my feelings about my life, the people in it, and my circumstances. Knowing this, I would be less consumed by trying to change my outer world and more interested in exploring my inner world.

Instead of giving you more tools, strategies, and techniques to follow, what I want to offer you are some of the insights and knowledge I have gained that changed for the better the way I see my life and myself. I really hope that you find in this book something that will be helpful to you; that there will be a chapter, a paragraph, or a sentence that will resonate with you on a deeper level.

I have no way of knowing if what I say in this book will have some kind of impact on you because I am not in control of that. But what I do quietly wish for is that you'll be left with a feeling: a good feeling, about yourself and about your life. And I hope you'll get curious about it and you will turn your attention inwards and explore that feeling.

I didn't write this book to convince you of my "truths" or to impose my ideas on you. It doesn't matter if what I say in this book is good (or not good) enough, right, or wise. You may think it is, or you may think that it isn't. After all, it is just another book, and I am just another person who decided to share with you how I see life and what I think it takes to make sure life doesn't suck.

I know that, had I known the things I will be sharing with you, many moments in my life, my relationships (including the one with myself), and many of my life choices would have been different. I am not suggesting that, had I known these things, life would be nothing but smooth sailing, and all I'd be doing all day every day was stopping to smell the roses. It doesn't mean that "bad" moments would not have happened and that life would not throw at me challenging situations. What I mean is that I would have viewed my life, myself, and my circumstances from a different, healthier and, let's just say a more chilled perspective. Because of that, all those "bad" times or difficult circumstances would suck much less or not at all.

What I truly desire is that once you put this book down, you'll care much less about what I or anyone write in their books and become more interested in listening to your own inner wisdom.

1

YOU DON'T HAVE TO CHANGE ANYTHING TO SEE EVERYTHING DIFFERENTLY.

We don't see things as they are.

We see everything through the filters made of our thoughts.

Let me tell you a story.

From about the age of seven, I used to think that my life mostly sucked. I won't be going into all the reasons why because I don't want to turn this chapter into a therapy session. But to give you some idea, I will say that I was raised in a so-called "dysfunctional family" where emotional turmoil was a normal part of daily life. The early years and then the teenage years often did not feel fun or carefree. My "ups" were really short, and my "downs" lasted far too long. I longed for inner peace far more than I longed for happiness. But when I look back, I can see how, despite all that was happening in my life and in my head, somehow, I never lost hope! Not only that, I somehow knew that I would not feel this way forever. I knew that I could and would feel at peace one day, and ever since, I have been trying to figure out how I could make it happen.

I began my research when I was seven years old — just kidding. I was in my late teens. I read a lot of books recommended by some of my friends who either were going to or had already studied psychology. Access to information was limited when I started. There was no Internet! And, once we did have the Internet, not everyone had WiFi at home or even a computer. Basically, for many years, if you wanted any information on any subject, you went to a library. Yes, that's how old I am. But fast forward. My quest continued when I left home and went to university. It continued when I moved abroad. And it continued when I went back to university to do my Ph.D. It was a long process. I was almost thirty when I began to find the answers I was seeking.

One day, I came across a book. I was about to go on vacation, and I was on Amazon looking for something interesting to read to take with me. There were quite a few self-help books that popped up on the screen. But that's not what I was looking for. I wasn't really into self-help books back then. I was earning my Ph.D.; I was an academic. So, of course, I would not be interested in the "pseudo-psychology for the masses," which is how I referred to self-help books back then. This sounds uptight, and I don't think I have ever been that type of person, but there is a lot of truth in the fact that "self-help" was largely ridiculed in academic circles. It's crazy when I think about it now because the people (myself included) who were most judgemental about those books had never read one (or certainly not many).

. . .

But this is what happens when we are not open-minded when we dismiss something out of hand without much knowledge about it. I was guilty of doing that myself. I did not read enough self-help books at the time to really have a well-informed opinion about them. But what I eventually read was not satisfying, as far as my quest for peace and happiness.

What these books seemed to convey, from my perspective, could be summed up this way: in order to be happy or to experience well-being, I would have to practice something, follow some steps, do exercises or apply various techniques. Or I could follow a disciplined spiritual practice to achieve my own enlightenment. I knew myself well enough to know that I was not disciplined enough to do the latter. I did try some exercises and techniques like changing my thoughts from negative to positive, but I found it all really mechanical and tedious. The results never lasted, and the idea that I would have to use techniques or tools in order to be happy and at peace for the rest of my life did not feel right; it didn't feel fun or sustainable. This is why I wasn't satisfied with the answers I found in self-help books.

But, returning to that day when I was looking for a book on Amazon, the one I felt really drawn to was a self-help book called You Can Have What You Want written by Michael Neill. I mean, come on! This was exactly the kind of self-help title I would avoid. But I bought it. I know it sounds weird, but I just knew I had to.

. . .

To this day, I am grateful that I did. That book literally marked the beginning of a whole new chapter in my life. More importantly, the book got me closer to the answers I was looking for. I will never forget the moment I sat with it and stared at the cover, the cover that proclaimed You Can Have What You Want. On the outside, my life looked great. On the inside, not so much. I had not even opened the book yet when the realization hit me like a ton of bricks: I had never asked myself: what do I truly want? I didn't have a clue.

I am not talking about the choice of a degree or a career, the house I would like to live in, or the places in the world I would like to visit. I am talking about my deepest desires. I am talking about everything I truly cared for. I am talking about what really mattered to me and what I was no longer willing to tolerate. The realization freaked me out. I was nearly thirty! Wasn't it too late for me to start figuring these things out? The answer is "no," in case you're wondering. There is no expiration date when it comes to you and your true desires, your wants, or your dreams!

Of course, at some point, I stopped staring at the cover. I opened the book and read it. But while the book helped me discover and learn a lot about myself, there was something else that really struck me as I was reading it. It was the tone of the book, the way it was written, and how I felt while reading it. I got curious and decided to find out more about the author.

I found his website and blog. I read a few of his articles; they were mostly about well-being, not so much about happiness. There were no steps or techniques to follow. I found them genuinely refreshing for this reason alone. All he talked about was our thoughts; how seeing them for what they are can change how we experience life, about how our minds work, and so on.

I did not understand much of what he was saying. I understood the words and sentences, of course. But I wasn't really getting what he was saying on a deeper level. I was curious, though. Very curious. In fact, I was so curious and eager to understand Michael's teachings that a month later, I was on the phone to him and, soon after that, he became my mentor for more than a year. During that same year, I completed a coaching course taught by Michael and other amazing teachers in Los Angeles, and I graduated with a Diploma of Transformative Coaching. Did I forget to mention that in the middle of pursuing my Ph.D. I decided to become a coach?

Because I was in the UK and Michael was in the US, we would not be able to meet in person every week, so we talked on the phone instead. You can imagine how excited I was, how grateful I felt that I was going to spend a year talking to this world-renowned coach and a best-selling HayHouse author! But my excitement began to fade quickly.

When I began to share all my problems and issues with Michael, it seemed to me he didn't want to talk about any of it. And I thought we would be talking about it all a lot! I thought we would be spending most of our time together, analyzing and solving all my problems. After all, wasn't it what coaching was for? As far as I was concerned, my issues and my problems stood in the way of my well-being and my eternal happiness.

Instead, I heard Michael repeat, again and again, this one sentence: It's just a thought. And you know what I thought? *Are you fucking kidding me?*

Excuse my French, but this is precisely how I reacted (in my head, that is). I was shocked and slightly angry, to be frank, because what I heard from Michael was so radically different from how I was used to seeing myself and my life right until that moment. And, trust me, it would have been very easy to dismiss it and think that what he was saying was simply ridiculous. But I decided to remain open-minded and take time to reflect on every piece of information that was new to me, and I would like to ask you to the same as you read on. Keep an open mind. Try not to read this book to agree or disagree, or to understand every single thing I say in it. Simply relax and read. When we're relaxed, the chatter in our heads settles. That's when we have new insights. Because truth be told, it is not the content of this book that will make a difference to you, but the time you spend reflecting on the things I will be talking about and your own unique insights that will.

It turned out that Michael's view about how our experience of life is created and where our feelings come from was very different than the view I had about it. His was the *inside-out* view. My view was definitely the *outside-in*. When he went on to explain his view (which is what I will do very soon), at first, I really struggled to grasp what he meant fully. I didn't agree with some of the things he was saying. That's because (I know now) I still wasn't really getting it. For quite a while, I could only understand what he was teaching intellectually, but I wasn't getting it on a deeper level.

. . .

You may be wondering what I mean when I talk about understanding something on a deeper level. Let me explain it briefly.

Imagine that you never saw a sunset in your life. I could explain to you what it looks like. I could tell you about all its different colors. I could explain to you why the Sun sets in the first place and about the Earth's rotation. And then I could tell you about the Earth itself, and the Sun's place in relation to the Earth and so on and so forth. I could tell you how I feel when I see the sunset and try to explain my experience of it. You would be really well informed and educated on the subject.

You would understand intellectually everything you learned about the sunset and think that you get it, that you get what it's like to experience the sunset. But that's all you'd end up with— an intellectual understanding—until you saw the sunset for yourself. Now, you'd have the experience. You'd feel what it's like to experience the sunset. It would be your own unique experience, and it would have nothing to do with theory.

There are many terms people use to describe these unique experiences. Some describe them as an "aha moment," or a "shift of consciousness/perspective/perception," an "inner knowing," an "awakening" or "epiphany." All those moments are intangible, but they feel meaningful and real to us. So, that's what I mean when I talk about understanding something on a deeper level. It's not something intellectual. It's experiential. It's a deeper feeling that goes hand in hand with a sense of clarity.

For quite some time during my work with Michael, I could only understand what he was telling me intellectually. There were times when I felt really frustrated because of it. But I wasn't going to give up. Despite my resistance to some of his ideas, deep down, I knew what he was saying was true. I really wanted to understand what he was pointing to. I wanted to know what that thing that felt true to me was.

One day I finally did. My circumstances did not change. The things I had found problematic until then were still present in my life. So were all the reasons I always thought stood in the way of my well-being and my happiness. And yet, everything looked very different to me. It was as if I had gained a new pair of eyes through which I viewed my life and my circumstances. But more importantly, I finally found the answers I had been seeking. And, for the first time in my life, I felt truly at peace.

I wasn't meditating when that moment happened. I wasn't sitting in the ashram or on the top of the mountain somewhere in India (although it would be really nice if I did). I was having lunch with Michael in Phoenix, Arizona. We were simply having a chat when that moment happened and when I saw myself and my life with fresh, new eyes. I had an insight that completely shifted my perspective.

All the problems and issues I thought I had to solve, change, or get rid of were still there, but they no longer looked like issues or problems. In fact, I saw very clearly that whether they were problems came down to my own thoughts. So, when I saw them without these thoughts, I no longer needed to solve or change anything. There was no drama and no sense of urgency to do something about my problems. I just knew that if and when

How To Make Sure Your Life Doesn't Suck 9

anything had to change, it would, and I would know when and how to do it.

I saw for the first time that how I experience life and everything in it has everything to do with my thoughts. I realized that we struggle only when we are caught up in our thoughts. We don't struggle when we have clarity about a situation, and we go with the flow of life with much more ease regardless of the circumstances. But when we are caught up in our thoughts, we go against the flow, and that's how we perceive a lot that is happening to us as a problem.

When we don't realize that how we feel has had everything to do with our thoughts, we innocently begin to associate how we feel with what's happening in our lives or with other people. I knew from then on, that's what human experience is like—we think and we always will—and there is no escape from it. We either navigate through life from the "caught up in our thinking" place or from a place of clarity and, throughout our lives, we continually shift between one and the other. But what makes life suck much less is the ability to recognize where we're at in any given moment and allow this awareness to guide us. We will talk more about that later on.

I understood, on a deeper level, that reality is what it is, but our experience of reality comes from our thoughts. I saw it clearly. I understood that I didn't have to change my thoughts or even how I felt to feel happier or more at peace. I didn't need my circumstances or people to change to feel better because happiness and well-being have very little to do with practices but with an awareness and understanding that all our feelings come from our thoughts, moment by moment.

I knew from then on that there would be ups and downs in my life because that's life.

I knew that life would be a fun ride and that there would always be times when the journey gets tough. But, with this new understanding I now gained, I knew I'd be alright regardless. Because it became very clear to me that how I feel and how I navigate through life has very little to do with what is happening to me or with the people around me, but everything to do with my thoughts.

As you can see, it was one hell of an "aha moment." And Michael told me later, he knew that I was experiencing a shift because a twinkle appeared in my eyes and my whole face lit up. (No, there were no angelic voices in the background, and no halo appeared over my head, in case you were wondering.)

2

WE EXPERIENCE LIFE FROM THE INSIDE-OUT.

Something wonderful begins to happen with the simple realization that life, like an automobile, is driven from the inside-out, not the other way around.

Richard Carlson

Let's begin from the *outside-in* versus *inside-out* view of reality. If you want to make sure your life doesn't suck, knowing about these two perspectives and understanding the differences between them is truly important. Then all it takes is a little bit of curiosity, a little bit of imagination, and a willingness to play with both perspectives. Willingness to explore how anything that happens in your day-to-day life would look through these two different lenses. Sooner or later, you'll begin to see the difference, naturally. Then you will start to feel it because you will begin to experience your life differently.

. . .

When we have the *outside-in* view of reality, we associate our feelings with external events and or people. Whatever we feel appears to be caused by something (an event, a circumstance, a situation) or by someone (what they said or what they did).

The *inside-out* view of reality means the exact opposite. It means that how we feel is generated from within via our thoughts. In other words, it is not an event, a situation, or a person "making" us feel good or bad (or any other feeling). It is what we think about that event, that situation or that person that determines how we feel and how we experience them.

More and more people are into personal growth or self-help. So, to many, it is nothing new that how we feel is a reflection of our thoughts. You may already know that too. There are hundreds of books that talk about this concept. There are hundreds of coaches and gurus who encourage us to change our thinking or to think positively.

Before I began to work with Michael, I knew this much too. But here's the thing: just because I knew I should think positive thoughts to have a positive experience or to feel good, it did not prevent me from feeling bad (anxious, insecure, depressed, etc.). And, of course, I didn't want to feel bad. But, at the time, I didn't know how I could change that. The idea that I would have to practice forever altering or observing my thoughts did not appeal to me at all. I kind of understood that my thoughts played an important role in how I experienced my life or in how I dealt with different circumstances. And yet, I still believed that a lot of what was happening to me on the outside had a lot to do with how I felt on the inside.

. . .

The most challenging part was to see that our experience of EVERYTHING in life comes from our thoughts, moment by moment. After a while, I realized that if people or circumstances were the cause of how we feel, then every single person on this planet would have to feel THE SAME way in response to the same person or to the same event. This realization, to me, made perfect sense.

And yet, upon further reflection, I began to question this logic. I began to think about people who were terminally ill, or who experienced war, or who were physically and emotionally abused. The idea that their emotional pain, sadness, or anger were caused by their thoughts and not by those events was something I really struggled to accept. In fact, I thought it was insensitive and borderline cruel even to suggest that it wasn't the events but their thoughts that were the cause of their pain. The *outside-in* view of reality completely made sense, to me, in those instances.

I spent a lot of time reflecting on this subject. I thought about all the people I knew who found themselves in all kinds of challenging situations. One of the first instances I looked at closely was the stories I heard or read about people diagnosed with cancer (or any terminal illness).

Upon reflection, I realized that although the same illness struck them, their experiences, and how they dealt with it differed from person to person. Some were really upset. They struggled to come to terms with what happened to them, and they would describe their experience as an ordeal or as a tragedy. Others talked about their cancer diagnosis as a life-changing experience. In fact, I remember how shocked I was when I heard some people say they were grateful for their illness because, despite the physical pain and everything else they had to deal with, they felt at peace.

They talked about how, because of their illness, they got in touch with who they really were. Or they said that, because of the illness, they understood what life was truly about and what was truly important. Others talked about their feelings changing constantly. One day they would feel sad or scared, but later they would feel fine and even happy. I saw clearly that even though they all had cancer, how they felt about it would be different from person to person. What they all had in common was the ability to experience anger and sadness, as well as moments, days, and even weeks when they would feel joy and peace.

I realized that when we look at any situation most of us would deem tragic or challenging from the *outside-in* perspective, we (innocently) do not recognize the capacity within each and every person to experience joy, love, peace of mind or well-being despite their circumstances.

Then I thought about all those who were abused as children, physically or emotionally, by those entrusted with their care. You might know them personally, or you might have experienced it yourself (as much as I hope you did not). Our childhoods are often seen as a major cause of depression or as a cause of our psychological struggles in adulthood. And a lot of people end up in therapy where their childhood is analyzed as a way to deal with their current problems and issues.

So I first looked at the "unhappy childhood" from the *outside-in* perspective because I was familiar with it. I used to "blame" my childhood for some of the issues I had. The books I read back then confirmed that there was, in fact, a correlation between my childhood and the issues and problems I had in my adulthood. And I actually felt relieved because there were many times in my life when I thought that something was wrong with me. I learned from those books that the feeling was normal and that it had everything to do with my childhood. I still thought there was something wrong with me, but now I had an explanation for it.

When I began to explore what my childhood would look like from the *inside-out* perspective, it occurred to me that if the "unhappy childhood" was the reason why we have problems and issues (mainly psychological), and why we feel unhappy at present; then everyone who had an "unhappy childhood" would have to have issues and feel unhappy in their adulthood.

I didn't have to look far to see that wasn't the case. My sister and I grew up in the same so-called "dysfunctional family," and we would certainly not describe our childhoods, in general, as happy and carefree. And yet, in many ways, how we feel about our childhood today is different. It appeared to me that it is not "the childhood" but rather the kind of thoughts we have about it today that determines how we feel about it. It even determines whether we make any correlation between what happened to us in the past with what is happening in our lives today.

. . .

I realized that we have to have unhappy thoughts (whether we are aware of those thoughts or not) about our childhood in order to feel unhappy. We have to think that our childhood is a problem for it to look that way. We have to think about our childhood and how we feel about it is a reflection of the kind of thoughts we have about it at any given moment.

This is why there are times when I think about my childhood, and I feel sad, or I feel pain. There are other times when I think about my childhood, and I smile. And there are times when what felt painful, scary, or awful when I was a child, now looks very different to me. Sometimes I even laugh at things I used to feel sad or angry about.

Today I know that it is OK to be experiencing all these feelings because I know that behind every feeling, there is a thought. It may be a thought about my childhood, but it is not my childhood that makes me feel one way or another. So, when I feel pain recalling some situations from my childhood, it is OK because I know this feeling comes from nothing but a thought at that moment. More importantly, just because I have painful thoughts and experience painful feelings does not mean that I am somehow broken or that there is something wrong with me.

Robert Kopecky articulated beautifully the point I am making here:

> *"All of us have known people who've been raised in pretty hellish*

situations, who then magically grow gardens of happiness and fulfilment out of the least likely plot of ground;

While others are born into very rich soil but seem to find themselves hopelessly locked out of the garden - forever banging on the door to get back in."

I understood that the *inside-out* perspective in relation to a "bad" or "unhappy" childhood isn't an attempt to question our experiences or facts about our childhood. It also does not imply that those who see their childhood as a problem are wrong, and those who don't are right, wiser, or more enlightened. There's no judgment. It simply allows us to recognize that we all have different thoughts. Because of that, we have different experiences and feel differently about our "unhappy" childhoods (or any event in our lives for that matter). Our childhood has nothing to do with how we feel currently. It has everything to do with our current thoughts about it—whether we are aware of those thoughts or not (more on that later).

I could share hundreds of stories about people who have lived through incredibly tough situations (or still are), who witnessed horrible things—things that none of us could even imagine—and yet how they experienced and responded to these situations was different from person to person. I don't want to do that here, but I would definitely encourage you to explore these stories so you can discover it for yourself.

It took me a while to understand that the *inside-out* view of reality points to the fact that our feelings and experiences of anything and anyone come from our thoughts. It does not question facts or events in our lives, and it doesn't judge how we feel about them. The *inside-out* understanding goes way beyond claims that how we feel and what we think is our choice. We don't think "on purpose." We simply think.

We live in a THOUGHT-created reality, which means we feel our thinking about life, people, and our circumstances. Whatever we feel changes moment by moment, day by day because our thoughts continuously change. This is why, no matter what circumstances we find ourselves in, we are able to experience all kinds of feelings.

It is why we can feel sad or insecure even when on the outside, our life looks really good; when it appears as though we have all the "reasons" to feel nothing but good. It is also why we can experience moments of joy and peace even when we feel at our lowest; when on the outside, it appears as though we have all the "reasons" to feel nothing but bad. It is why one moment we can feel really good only to feel low in a matter of seconds on any given day.

In the next chapter, I would like to share with you how I went from being completely unaware of the role our thoughts play in how we experience life to realizing that we live in a THOUGHT-created reality all the time. Moment by moment. Day by day. I want to show you how and why the moment we see that and understand the nature of what is happening; it fundamentally changes the way we look at life and ourselves.

3

OUR THOUGHTS AND OUR FEELINGS ARE NOT AS BIG OF A DEAL AS WE'RE USED TO THINKING

We experience our thinking as real to us.

It appears as a fact rather than what it is - just a transitory thought.

We misunderstand its role, attaching too much importance to our thinking and in doing so, turn it into a force with far too great an influence.

Terry Rubenstein

I quite like to think of life as a journey. We all go through different stages, and often a different stage means a different perspective from which we view life and ourselves. When I look back at my own journey, I can see how I have gone through three distinct stages, and I would like to tell you a little bit about them.

In the first one, I looked at life from the outside-in perspective. Life, people, places, and circumstances had everything to do with how I felt. It wasn't an idea, a belief, or a concept to me. It wasn't how I chose to see life. This was how I saw life. This is how life worked from my perspective. My well-being depended on other people and my circumstances. I was not aware that I had thoughts about those people and those circumstances, and that those thoughts had anything to do with how I felt. So life felt pretty "heavy" more often than not. From where I stood, I'd have to do a lot in my outside world in order to feel happy and at peace in my inner world. Either way, life was happening to me, and I'd just have to roll with the punches.

In the second stage, I still looked at life from the outside-in perspective, but now I'd enter the world of personal growth and self-help. At the time, I was feeling up and down quite a lot, and because of that, I thought there was something wrong with me. I wanted to stay up longer, and when I was down, I wanted it to change as quickly as possible. So I began my quest with one question in mind: "How can I feel happy?" (preferably most of the time).

I came across tonnes of information about how to change my thinking, how to prevent it, observe it, or reframe it so I could feel good as often as possible. Based on what I learned, one thing was certain - my THOUGHTS and my FEELINGS were really important, and if I wanted to be happy and at peace, I had to work on those thoughts and feelings. So, I went from being unaware of the role my thinking played in my life in stage one to being very aware of it in stage two. Often to the point of being freaked out about it because I now learned that I had control over my thoughts, and I should learn how to control them. This sounded like a lot of hard work and, if I failed to control my thoughts or think positive, my happiness and well-being were at stake. No pressure!

How To Make Sure Your Life Doesn't Suck

. . .

Either way, most of the literature I came across left no room for the possibility that it was OK to feel bad, to feel low, scared, or insecure. Instead, it innocently perpetuated the idea that a "positive state of mind" is a thing. That it can be permanent, and it can be achieved as long as I apply certain tools or techniques, or follow some step-by-step strategies. It didn't sound like fun to me, and it didn't seem sustainable.

This is not to say that I have not learned anything of value or that none of it was helpful. Everything I read helped me discover that there was more to life than what I was able to see in stage one. It made me curious and eager to learn more about life, about how it works, and about who I was. I just had that feeling that there was "more" and that everything I had learned thus far was only touching the surface of what I was yet to discover. This was the beginning of stage three, when I came across the inside-out understanding. It is where I am today. It's an ongoing process of exploration and new insights.

In the previous chapters, I shared with you my story and how, with time, I began to see more and more the inside-out nature of reality. That alone was a true eye-opener. But what made this stage so different and fundamentally changed the way I see life and myself was when I finally understood on a deeper level that we live in a THOUGHT-created reality. Not sometimes but ALL THE TIME, which means that we feel our thinking moment by moment, day by day.

I realized that how we feel about people reflects the thoughts we have about those people, good or bad. How we feel about ourselves reflects the thoughts we have about ourselves, good or bad. How we feel about our circumstances reflects the thoughts we have about our circumstances, good or bad. How we feel about money reflects the thoughts we have about money, good or bad. How we feel about failure reflects the thoughts we have about failure, good or bad. I could go on.

It was through this insight that I was able to see life and everything in it with no thoughts attached. The view was neutral, and all I was able to experience at that moment was clarity and peace of mind. I saw THOUGHT as creative energy that has nothing to do with us, and we have no control over it, which was the exact opposite of what I had learned previously.

I saw the transient nature of this energy, and that all our thoughts are nothing but forms that are made of that energy. This is why our thoughts come and go. They change whether we are aware of it or not. This is also why our feelings and moods change a lot. It also explains why we're able to experience a whole range of feelings on any given day and why we are capable of having moments of clarity, peace of mind, and joy even in those times when we feel at our lowest.

What I realized is that we are not in control of this process. In fact, I saw very clearly how any attempt to control it would be absolutely futile. All I had to do was to allow for this process to take place without my interference by trying to resist some thoughts, fight them, observe them, or change them. When I saw this transient nature of thought, from that moment on, I knew that I did not have to be afraid of my thoughts, and if I did not have to be afraid of my thoughts, I did not have to be afraid of my feelings. In fact, from that moment on, my thoughts or my feelings on any given day no longer matter to me as much as they used to.

I saw how everything in our lives comes from THOUGHT. All ideas, concepts, and all our beliefs are made of the same thing. This means that everything is up for questioning. The more we begin to see that, the closer we get to discover how everything we think about life and ourselves is made up, and by seeing that we get closer to discovering who we truly are. We discover that we are not our thoughts. We discover our natural OK-ness and our natural capacity to experience well-being. And, the less we pay attention to our thoughts and our feelings, the more we get to experience peace of mind regardless of what is going on in our lives.

Prior to my insight, I would pay a lot of attention to how I felt. I would look for the reasons why I felt one way or another. Or I would pay attention to my thoughts. Because I learned that I had to pay attention to them, try to change them, observe them, or control them. At the time, I saw thoughts as something tangible, something concrete that I could, in fact, do something about. The "hunt" for my thoughts, and my attempts to change them were pretty exhausting. So was trying to change how I felt whenever I felt bad.

All my life, I thought that my feelings were important, and a lot of literature out there would confirm that. I felt as though all my life, I have been waging a battle with my feelings. Whenever I felt anxious, insecure, or scared, I'd try to fight those feelings or get rid of them. I wasn't aware that the more I fight them, the longer they persist. More on that later.

So, it was a huge relief when I realized I didn't have to do anything about my thoughts other than letting them come and go and not freak out as soon as I began to feel anxious, stressed or insecure. I saw THOUGHT as this powerful creative energy and thoughts as paintbrushes delivering all kinds of pictures to our awareness moment by moment. This is why some days we get scary pictures and feel scared, and some days we get happy pictures and feel happy. But what makes a huge difference is knowing that we can relax and not be as freaked out by what we're feeling, in particular, when the pictures we get look really scary.

Discovering the transient nature of thought was a real game-changer. I did not realize that we think all the time. In fact, some scientists claim that we have tens of thousands of thoughts each and every day and that a "thought travels 930,000 times faster than the sound of our voice ." Don't ask me how they know that. The bottom line is that we simply cannot be aware of all of them because, if we were, we'd all go crazy and our heads would probably explode. This is why we are only aware of some of our thoughts.

Let's do a little experiment.

I would like you to pause for a moment and become aware of your breathing.

. . .

Have you done that? Thanks!

I am pretty sure that right before I asked you to do that, you were not even aware that you have been breathing all along. Which means that just because you were not aware of your breathing doesn't mean that there was no breathing going on, right?

The same process takes place when it comes to our thoughts. Thoughts come and go all the time. But, most of the time, we are not aware of that. This is important because when we are not aware that there's a whole lot of thinking happening "behind the scenes" moment by moment, we begin to associate how we feel with external circumstances, other people, or events that take place in our lives. But, the moment we remember that we live in a THOUGHT-created reality, it doesn't matter whether we are aware of our thoughts or not. There's no need to "hunt" for them or analyze them.

The moment we remember that behind every feeling (good or bad), there is nothing but a transient thought (or a bunch of thoughts) we no longer have to be afraid of how we feel. The need to know why we feel one way or another suddenly drops. So is the need to change or fight our thoughts and our feelings. We don't "go there" because we know that all we are setting ourselves up for are just more and more thoughts. In fact, as soon as you feel low, it can be your clue that it is NOT the time to analyze your thoughts or to wonder why you feel low. More on that later.

. . .

The more we begin to see the transient nature of our thoughts, the sooner we begin to relax as if by default. We stop freaking out as soon as we feel anxious, insecure, or lost. We're less attached and consumed by our thoughts and our feelings, and, because of that, we begin to experience more well-being. With less noise in our heads, we naturally become more present. And, when we are more present, we become more creative, more productive, and, best of all, more in tune with our intuition. When we don't pay attention to our thoughts, we get to hear, more and more, the whispers of our inner wisdom - the best navigation system we all have - and we let it guide us each and every day.

Our relationship to how we feel at any given moment changes because we realize that whatever we're feeling is temporary, and we're always only one thought away from feeling differently. Eventually, we begin to embrace our human experience in its entirety. Which means we stop trying to change it or fight it. We embrace moments of joy and happiness. We embrace moments of grief and sadness. Deep down, we know that beneath all those experiences, we are truly well, and because of that, we are able to deal with anything that life brings with much more grace and ease.

Have you noticed how we are naturally capable of embracing the weather, whatever it may be on any given day? We may not like cold or rainy days, but we accept them. We understand that weather changes and sometimes really often depending on where we live. We don't try to change the weather. We don't fight it. We don't try to manipulate it. Of course, we have our preferred weather, but have you noticed how even that differs from person to person? Either way, we live our lives. We don't stay at home just because the weather is terrible. We don't pay too much attention to what the weather is like. We don't care so much when it ill will change or when the rain will pass. All we know is that it will pass.

Our feelings change just like the weather. When our thoughts change, our feelings change too. Our moods change. It all comes and goes. But when we understand the very nature of what is happening, we begin to be less attached and consumed by our personal "storms" and "clouds." Because of that, we're able to experience more well-being regardless of what our personal "weather" is like at any given moment.

4

DON'T BE PREOCCUPIED WITH THE "WHY."

There is nothing you can do to quiet the mind faster than doing nothing to quiet the mind.

Michael Neill

Listen. I know that when we feel low or when we are in a bad mood, we almost automatically want to change it. Of course, we do not want to feel anxious, scared, or insecure. It is perfectly normal that, when we feel those feelings, we look for solutions, tips, or advice that would help us get back to feeling good again. I understand that.

Even though I know that whatever I feel at any moment is a reflection of the thoughts I'm thinking at that moment, when I feel low, I often tend to forget that. And you know why? Because having this understanding does not stop us from being human and getting caught up in our thinking.

. . .

The *inside-out* view simply helps us understand our human experience so that we can feel more chilled about our feelings and emotions. We can have a healthy distance to what's happening in our heads. We can experience our well-being more often, even when we face the challenges life brings. Ultimately, we can actually feel more comfortable being human!

I do feel low, I get scared, I feel anxious, I feel insecure. My moods go up and down too. And I do absolutely nothing to change how I feel. Because even though it often seems that I feel bad because someone said something or because something happened (or didn't happen), deep down, I know that it is not true. I know that I'm simply caught up in my thinking. I don't go into the content of my thinking; I do not think about my thoughts; I do not analyze my thoughts or observe them. I basically do whatever occurs to me to do. I do anything BUT wonder why I feel the way I feel!

I know how counterintuitive and even ridiculous this approach may sound in comparison to all the practices out there designed to help escape any "bad" feeling. After all, psychologists, therapists, and some coaches encourage us to do the exact opposite. They focus on the content of our thoughts and on the analysis. But what I love about this approach is that it is simple.

I believe that good advice is simple advice. There are sayings that were born out of the wisdom of ordinary people, who somehow knew that when we feel low or grapple with any problem, we should "sleep on it" or "put it on a back burner."

Somehow they knew that if we try hard to find a solution or to change how we feel, the opposite happens. We don't see any solution, and we feel even more frustrated and bad about it.

Here's what I know, and what most of us can relate to.

You know when we cannot recall someone's name? The more we think about it, and no matter how hard we're trying to figure out what this name is, it doesn't make us any wiser because we still cannot remember the name. Not only that, we get more and more frustrated or angry. If we do something else, we don't think about it anymore. Then the name pops in our head, as if out of the blue.

Here's why it happens.

The moment we occupy ourselves with any task, we stop thinking about the "name." Because of that, our thoughts dissipate naturally, and that creates a space in our heads for a fresh thought to occur. It's this new thought that brings the answer. Because our mind isn't busy anymore, we calm down naturally. So, we not only have the answer or a solution, but we also are back in touch with our well-being.

I know the more I try to figure anything out, the more I will be thinking about it, and I will only become more confused or overwhelmed. And then I will have more thoughts about how it sucks that I can't figure it out and more thoughts about what that means about me.

. . .

I know when my mind is busy, there's no space for a fresh thought to appear. Which means there is no space for a new idea or a new insight to occur. So, I leave it. Literally. Because I know that I cannot force a fresh thought with more thinking. How do we know that our minds are busy? The clues are our feelings. You can be sure that when you experience feelings such as resistance, stuckness, stress, overwhelm, a sense of urgency, anxiety, etc. that's how you know. And that's all you need to know.

If I pay any attention to how I feel whenever I'm in a low mood, I am actually preventing this low feeling from passing, naturally. If I pay attention to how I feel, I will start analyzing and looking for the reasons why I feel the way I feel, why I feel stressed, anxious, stuck, overwhelmed, etc. And you know what? I will find not one, but probably multiple "reasons" why I feel low. And they will ALL feel very compelling, especially when I'm in a low mood. And, once there, it's very easy to forget that it is my thinking that is creating it! Now I have "reasons" to feel this way! Now I don't just feel low. Now, because I have "reasons," I begin to think about those reasons, and I find myself in what feels like a deep mental shit storm!

I highly recommend that you don't do that. Don't analyze. Don't "go there." You will always find something that feels compelling enough to be the "reason" why you feel bad. Instead, recognize that you feel bad and move on. Go do something else. Ignore it. Or do nothing at all.

. . .

It doesn't matter. What matters is that you don't attach any importance to how you feel. As soon as you use the word because that's how you'll end up on a slippery slope. As soon as you say: I feel bad, depressed, anxious, scared BECAUSE... [fill the blank], you're on a roll. That's how you end up generating a mental shit storm.

I once was introduced to the idea that whenever I feel low, I should observe my thoughts in a detached way and let them pass. I am not suggesting that this approach is right or wrong, because perhaps I have not understood well how it is supposed to work. It didn't work for me. And when it didn't work, I felt bad that I was not able to achieve that kind of detached state.

One day it occurred to me that trying to observe my thoughts when I feel low while, at the same time, trying to remain detached from them would be like sitting on the beach in the middle of a hurricane and observing the storm waves — then trying to select those waves (thoughts), which made me feel most scared while at the same time trying to remain detached and not afraid of them. I realized that it would be much wiser to just get up, go do something else and let the hurricane pass. It would save me a lot of time and energy I would otherwise spend on trying to remain detached and unafraid.

The bottom line is this: if you don't pay attention to your thoughts—don't analyze them, observe them, or try to get rid of them—your mind and your thoughts will settle all on their own, and you will be able to experience clarity and well-being again.

. . .

How To Make Sure Your Life Doesn't Suck

I know that there are tools and techniques that people use to quiet their minds. If you use any of these techniques and it works for you, by all means, continue. Even though I cannot offer you another tool, there is something that I find incredibly helpful. I want to share it with you.

I know that you and I and every human on this planet have this amazing built-in mechanism that allows our minds and thoughts to settle on their own. To show you how it works, I'd like you to think of a snow globe. Imagine that the globe is your mind, and the snowflakes in it are your thoughts.

When you overthink, when you analyze your thoughts or begin to wonder why you feel what you feel at any given moment, when you try to change them or manipulate them in any way, by doing any of these things, you are shaking up the snow globe. The snowflakes will float around. They will fill up the whole bubble. There will be more and more of them the more you shake it.

You created a snowstorm. You don't get to see the little figurines inside the bubble. It's the same when we are caught up in our thoughts. We cannot experience clarity, and we feel detached from our well-being.

But the moment we put the snow globe down and leave it alone, the snowflakes will start to fall, and the storm will settle all on its own. We'll be able to see the figurines that were there all along when we go back to look at it later. We will be able to experience the well-being again, or see something new when we leave our thoughts and feelings alone.

I don't do anything to quiet my mind actively. I simply remember that I have this amazing mechanism inside that will take care of it, so I don't have to do anything about it. I simply remember that the less attention I pay to how low or bad I feel at any moment, the quicker I'm going to snap out of that feeling, naturally. The more I pay attention to how I feel or wonder why, the longer the crappy feeling will persist.

The best advice I heard was that of a wise man who said, "So!" Even though it had nothing to do with feelings, I loved it because something occurred to me when I read it. If every time I feel bad, I said to myself: "So!" it would probably do wonders. I would see, at that moment, that how I feel isn't important. I would not freak out about feeling bad. Instead, I would probably laugh.

OK. Enough about feeling bad! Let's talk about feeling goooooood!

When we leave our feelings and thoughts at peace, sooner or later, we'll bounce back to feeling good. It often happens suddenly. It happens so naturally that we might not even notice when we stopped feeling bad and started feeling good. This is one of the reasons we can't remember why we were so angry or upset a few hours or a few days ago. We might remember that we argued with someone or had a little meltdown, but we struggle to figure out what the fuss was about.

How To Make Sure Your Life Doesn't Suck

. . .

Just like our bad feelings, our good feelings reflect our thoughts. The very same mechanism applies here. We feel good thoughts, and we feel good. And we might be aware that we think good thoughts or we might not be aware that we're thinking at all.

And here's the thing. When we forget that our good feelings reflect our thoughts at any moment, we begin to associate our good feelings with something or someone. Yet again we have the *outside-in* view of reality, because we think that our happiness and well-being have something to do with what we do (the job we have, the vacations we go on), what we have (house, car, money, fame), what we achieve (our goals, the tasks we manage to complete, the exams we pass) or with other people (our parents, our partners, and our relationships in general).

Sometimes, it appears as though the moment we find a solution to any problem, it is this solution that changes how we feel. For example, when we struggle with money, it appears as though it is the lack of money that makes us feel anxious or stressed. We are unaware, or we forget that how we feel about this situation has everything to do with the type of thoughts we have about money and about ourselves. When the money is there because we got a new job, we borrowed the money or won a lottery we begin to feel good. It appears as though having the money had changed the way we feel. What we don't realize is the reason why we feel good is that we're no longer caught up in our thoughts about the lack of money. We begin to think about something else.

. . .

It is very easy to fall into the *outside-in* view of reality when we forget that our thoughts about everything create our feelings moment by moment. In those moments, it appears as though when something changes for the better on the outside, it also changes how we feel on the inside.

When we can't see that our happiness or well-being (and any positive feelings) are generated from within, we think if we do more, achieve more, and have more, we will be happy. But what tends to happen is we end up feeling good for a bit, and we might even have a sense of satisfaction. But these feelings soon fade away (because that's what feelings do), and we wonder why we are not happy, again. Why, even though we have all the stuff and we achieved whatever we wanted to achieve, we still don't feel happy, and all we're left with is this feeling that something is still missing. What do we do? We set new goals. We buy more stuff. We achieve more.

Or we sign up for seminars and workshops. Or we reach for self-help books. I am glad that we have the seminars and the books if they help us to discover who we really are. What I don't like about what's said during some of those seminars or in some self-help books, is that we need to DO more to be happy. That we need techniques, tools, and strategies, or other practices to experience well-being. That we need fixing. That we need to make self-improvement our life mission. That we need to go to more seminars and read more books to feel at peace. In this way, they perpetuate the idea that our happiness and well-being are somewhere "out there," that the answers we need are to be found in books or at the seminars, rather than within ourselves.

. . .

And I want to tell you this.

You are OK! Whether you feel good or not so good at the moment, you are OK! Whatever is happening in your life right now, you are OK! The only thing that stands in the way of you seeing that is a thought. Not your circumstances, not what you do for a living, not how you look, or how much money you have. It's just a thought.

Thoughts are like clouds that cover the Sun. Just because we cannot see the Sun through the clouds, it does not mean it is not there! In fact, we know it is there! It's been there all along, no matter how long the dark clouds (thoughts) have been hovering over our heads. Just like the Sun, all the answers you need and all the peace you can have are already here. They are within you!

The more you look within and not somewhere else for the answers, the quicker you will see it and experience it for yourself. The less attention you pay to the "clouds," the quicker they will start to fade away, and what you feel at any given moment won't be that relevant. Because now you'll know that whatever you feel is made of thoughts. And thoughts come and go. They are temporary. So are your feelings.

Instead, you will discover that it is perfectly OK that sometimes you feel scared and sometimes you feel courageous. That sometimes, you feel confident, and sometimes you feel insecure. That sometimes, you feel certain, and sometimes you feel lost. That sometimes you feel really bad, and sometimes you feel really good. That sometimes, you feel proud of yourself, and sometimes you feel like a failure. That sometimes, you feel you could conquer the world, and sometimes you feel you're a loser. That sometimes, you feel that life is unfair, and sometimes you feel that life is beautiful. That sometimes, you feel like you want to end it all, and sometimes you feel grateful that you are alive.

Whatever you feel is made of thoughts. However, you see yourself is made of thoughts too.

And YOU are NOT your thoughts. What you think about yourself has nothing to do with who you truly are at your core, and at your core, you are whole. You can have all kinds of thoughts about who you are and what you are capable of, but those thoughts change constantly. You are not and cannot be permanently insecure, depressed, uncertain, anxious, happy, stressed, ecstatic, confident, lost, courageous, and so on.

Our thoughts are like costumes we get to wear throughout our lives. These costumes may change how we appear (to ourselves and others), but they do not change who we are underneath. It doesn't matter if the costume is pretty, ugly, or scary. You wouldn't be afraid if you saw yourself in the mirror while wearing a scary Halloween costume, would you? Maybe for a moment. That's OK. But it wouldn't bother you because you'd know that it is just a costume, and that underneath is the real you.

Every costume you wear is nothing but a reflection of your thoughts. It can be an "anxious costume," an "insecure costume,"

How To Make Sure Your Life Doesn't Suck

or a "happy costume." You may wear it for a day, for a month, or years. Sometimes when you wear a certain costume for a really long time, you get used to it, you get used to a role, and you forget who you truly are is underneath it.

When you think good thoughts, your costume will look pretty to you, and you will feel comfortable wearing it. But when you think bad thoughts, your costume won't look pretty to you, and you will feel uncomfortable. You may want to change it or do something to make it more comfortable or to get rid of it altogether. You may try to beautify it (think positive) or get rid of the ugliest bits. But all you'd be doing are alterations. All you'd be changing is the surface.

This is why, sooner or later, you won't be happy about your costume again. You will try to do something about it. Until one day, you realize it is just a costume, and it is not a big deal, whether it is ugly or pretty. And that we humans get to wear all kinds of costumes throughout our lives. The costumes are never the problem; the problem begins when we don't recognize they are just costumes and then attach too much importance to them.

Beyond the thoughts, you think, and beyond what you feel, you are this perfectly whole being. You don't need to improve it or fix it. This is who you truly are! You are the infinity of awesomeness! And you have an infinite potential to see yourself with fresh new eyes. You have an infinite potential to create the kind of life you dream about!

5

EXCHANGE YOUR "BLAME DETECTOR" FOR THE "MOOD DETECTOR" AND SEE WHAT HAPPENS.

I have many moods, and there is no objective reality. I kind of live by that.

Juliana Hatfield

As obvious as it may sound, we have moods. Our moods can change quickly and frequently. Our moods reflect our thoughts. When we think gloomy thoughts, we find ourselves in a gloomy mood. When we think good thoughts, we find ourselves in a good mood. You may already know that. But even though I know that too, I still forget that my moods are like filters through which I view everything and everyone around me. What mood I am in on any given day will determine how I perceive anyone or anything, and how I will react to what's happening around me. But when I forget that, it seems like it is something else, something external that is spoiling or creating my good mood that day. My "blame detector" is definitely on in those moments, and I begin to look for something or someone to blame.

Let's take London, where I live, as an example of this phenomenon so you can see what I am talking about and relate it to your own experiences.

I love London. I love the buzz of the city. I love people watching. I even enjoy commuting and queueing up to get on a crowded London Tube (subway). Even though I don't live in central London, I live very close. And there are days when I think how awesome it is that I can just hop on a train and reach the city in no time. But there are days when I hate London. All of a sudden, I find everything annoying: people who walk too slowly, people who bump me and don't say "sorry," the Tube is too hot and crowded, or I can't find a seat, and I have to stand on my feet all the way home.

Can you see what's going on here?

If my "mood detector" were on, I would know that London has nothing to do with how I feel about London. London is always there. So are the people. So is the crowded Tube. London cannot change from one day to the next. But my experience of it can! And it does change; it can be different from one day to the next, and it can even change on the same day. I can love London in the morning, but in the afternoon I might hate it again! How I experience, London depends on the mood I am in that day.

. . .

What I'd like you to know is that the fact that we have moods and that they can change a lot is perfectly normal. Just because your moods go up and down, it doesn't mean that there's something wrong with you. And it certainly does not mean that you have some kind of mental condition, or that as soon as you feel a bit low, you need therapy or should be given an antidepressant.

What most of us are not aware of is how much of what sucks in our day-to-day lives is related to our moods and not the places we go, the situations we encounter, or the people whose paths we cross. To many, this realization comes as a shock. They are used to blaming everything and everyone for screwing up their day, their week, or their lives. When people really understand the role their moods play, it is a real eye-opener because they no longer see themselves as victims of what is happening to them.

When we are not aware that our moods reflect our thoughts, on any given day and in any circumstances, we begin to associate them with something or someone else. For example, it may appear to you as though what Joe in the office said has spoiled your mood. But, if you look back in time, you will be able to see that Joe may have said many things in the past, even things that could have been annoying, insulting, or hurtful. And yet, the way you took what he said and how you reacted, varied depending upon your mood at the time.

There would be days when you could not have cared less about what Joe said. You would brush it off. You would ignore it. Maybe you'd roll your eyes and simply walk away. Other times, you'd think he was a jerk, but you would not take it personally.

And then, there'd be times when what Joe said would piss you off and maybe even hurt you. But there would also be times when you'd be able to see through Joe's bullshit and see a man who was actually not too happy. You'd be able to see that something was up with him and that it would explain his behavior. In fact, you might even have compassion for Joe.

There's another scenario. Joe might have also said some nice things to you on a few occasions. And one day, you might have thought that it was nice of him. Maybe you even told him that he "made your day." But there would be days when you thought that he was dishonest or that whatever he said, he only did that because he probably needed something. Whatever the scenario, the bottom line is this: Joe could have said anything, but it is the mood you'd be in that day that would determine how you'd perceive and respond to what he had said.

However you react, whether you take what Joe says personally or brush it off, it's ALL OK, and it's all very human. I am only pointing out that our moods play a significant role in how we navigate through our daily lives and how we respond to people and situations. I am making zero judgment about how you should or should not react or behave, and I am not suggesting that you should "work on" your moods! I am only saying that how we perceive what is said, and how we react is down to our moods and not down to our friend, Joe. It's simply about having this awareness.

We can replace "Joe" with pretty much anyone and anything: the email we received that day, the weather, the train that arrived late, the news we heard on our way to work, the trash still sitting there because our partner forgot to take it out again, the Republicans, the Labour Party, the cat we tripped over, a bad cup of coffee, someone looking at us the "the wrong" way and what we think it means, the amount of likes under our Facebook post, what he said, what she said and so forth.

Just because it appears to us that anything or anyone is responsible for our moods, it is not the case. Sometimes we remember that and sometimes we forget it. We should not be too preoccupied with the fact that we have moods and that we may feel up and down often. Our thoughts change moment by moment, whether we are aware of it or not. When our thoughts change, our moods change. Life simply sucks less when we are aware of the role our moods play in how we go about it day-to-day.

One way you can become more aware is to reflect on different situations or events that took place in your life and see the way you felt and responded to them. Or you can reflect on what someone said to you in the past and how you felt and responded to what was said. I would like you to focus on instances when you reacted differently to similar situations.

Let me give you some examples.

Let's say your partner is meant to be taking the rubbish (trash) out (you can replace rubbish with any other household chores). And, sometimes he (or she) does that, and sometimes he (or she) forgets. I would like you to focus on how your feelings and your responses have been different throughout your relationship. Pay attention to what mood you were in or how you felt in those moments.

How about when a train or a plane you were waiting for was late or canceled? Have you always felt about it and reacted to it the same way?

Let's say you received feedback at work or in school, and it wasn't what you expected. OK, it was bad. Look at as many such instances as you can and, again, pay attention to what mood you were in the moment and how you then reacted. Did you feel and react to it the same way each time it happened?

The more examples you can find from your own life, the better you will be able to see the important role our thoughts play in how we experience life. I can give you more examples and talk more about any subject I raise in this book, but nothing will replace your own stories and your own examples. They are relatable to you, and it is what you discover for yourself when you explore them that will be most impactful.

6

ALWAYS MAKE YOUR BED AND DO IT WELL, OR ELSE!

But let there be spaces in your togetherness,

And let the winds of the heavens dance between you.

Khalil Gibran

In the previous chapter, we talked about the role our moods play in our day-to-day lives. In this chapter, I would like to focus on our relationships because whether our relationships suck or not has a lot to do with our moods too. How we feel about our partners or anything that goes on in our relationships depends on our thoughts. Our moods, good or bad, are a reflection of those thoughts. But, when we are not aware of that or simply forget that, we tend to blame our partners for how we feel. This is how we innocently end up creating a lot of unnecessary issues and problems.

. . .

None of us really likes to argue and, I think it's fair to say that pretty much everyone would like to be in a happy relationship. Many people read books and listen to relationship experts, either because they want to improve their relationships or because they may be experiencing some problems, and they would like to know how they could fix them. Many experts will say that communication is very important. That communication is the key to a happy relationship, and it can solve a lot of problems. I agree with that.

But good communication alone isn't the only key to a happy relationship. Our moods play a much greater role. They are like filters through which we perceive our partners and everything that happens in our relationships. They influence the way two people communicate, how they see each other, how they view their problems and issues, how they react, how they behave, and how they feel about anything that goes on in their relationships.

When we know this, our moods can become our personal navigation system that guides us and tell us when (and when not) to communicate. When two people in a relationship understand the role their moods play, they soon learn that when they communicate is more important than how they communicate with each other. They are able to distinguish when the "mood" is speaking and when it's not.

Whatever our partners say or however they behave when in a low mood, we won't be taking it too personally. We will be less reactive or argumentative. This understanding alone has made a huge difference in my own relationships, and it has helped save many couples from breakups and divorces. Or it simply helped many couples to be much happier in their relationships.

The moment we realize how much of what's going on in our relationships comes down to our moods (as opposed to "real" problems and issues), we are able to avoid a lot of arguments, conflicts, and drama. We are able to see that whatever we consider being "an issue" on any given day has everything to do with our moods and very little (or nothing) to do with our partner or the state of our relationship.

Now, I am not suggesting our partners are saints, and they always behave perfectly. I am not suggesting that we should tolerate behaviors that are unacceptable or abusive. Life brings all kinds of challenges that we may have to deal with as a couple. What I am saying is the way we experience and perceive what's happening, and how we respond to it comes down to our moods.

Whenever we find ourselves in a low mood (angry mood, sad mood, stressed mood, anxious mood, insecure mood, etc.), it simply means that we are caught up in our thoughts. Our minds are busy, and we lack clarity. We tend to be reactive, and we take things personally. How we perceive and respond to anything that goes on in our relationship on any given day is very different from how we'd perceive it and respond to it when in a good mood. When we're less caught up in our thoughts, we are calmer. We have more clarity. The ability to recognize where we're at on any given day allows us to make better choices and better decisions about whether something needs to change, or if we want to stay in or end the relationship.

. . .

When we don't know how much of what's happening in our relationships can be attributed to our moods, we tend to hold our partners responsible for how we feel. We blame them. We are convinced what they said or did "made" us feel insecure, angry, or sad. We feel so strongly about it, and we don't even consider another possibility. But there is another possibility, and I would like to use an example from my own relationship to illustrate that.

There's been an ongoing issue in my relationship for quite some time. I used to get really angry about it. You may or may not see it as an "issue" and think, "what's the big deal," but that alone shows you when we have an issue, it feels very real to us. It doesn't matter if others see it the same way.

My issue was the "unmade bed" or "bed not made properly." My partner would either not make our bed or make it in such a way that, as far as I was concerned, he might as well have left it unmade. It looked like a mess! And it would drive me mad. I would have a lot of thoughts going on in my head about it. The following are some of the thoughts I would have. You can imagine what mood I'd been in having those kinds of thoughts! Here we go:

"Why can't he make the bed properly? He knows how I like it to be. He knows that it annoys me when he does that. It really doesn't take much time or effort to do it properly. I showed him how it should be done many times. So it means when it's not done that way, he doesn't give a shit. He doesn't care how I feel and how important it is for me that he makes the freaking bed properly. And, if he doesn't care about me or my feelings, then what does it say about our relationship?"

So then I would feel angry or sad because I thought he didn't care. In short, I'd be in a really bad mood! Now, it wasn't just a "bed" issue; it became a "relationship" issue, and my partner was, of course, to blame for it.

Now, imagine my partner coming home on a day like that. Remember that in his mind, at that very moment, he has no idea what's been going on in my head. So, when he enters the house, all he sees is the end product of my thoughts—my face looking as if I wanted to kill him. He definitely won't hear me say, "Hi, Darling, how was your day?" Oh, no! But he will definitely hear about "the bed," even before he manages to take his shoes off.

Then, he will hear how he doesn't give a shit. Which means he doesn't care about my feelings. Forget my feelings. He doesn't care about me! And what does that say about him and about our relationship? Then he'd probably see me go to the kitchen where I would wash the dishes frantically. Or he'd see me grab my bag and leave for the gym where I wouldn't be doing yoga, oh no. I would be boxing! All the while, he'd be left there, unsure as to what the hell just happened and where it all came from.

Just as my mood played a huge role that day, his mood would play a role too. Because if he came home in a low mood, he would take my behavior personally. He would be pissed off.

He'd think all kinds of things about me and how I did not even let him take his shoes off first before I lashed out and blamed him for everything.

But if he came home in a good mood, he'd see almost instantly that I must have been in a low mood. He might wonder if I was actually OK. He'd look past the "bed" and everything else I said. He'd be able to see clearly that it was my "mood" speaking and not me! He'd get changed and watch TV. And, when I returned, he'd probably give me a hug.

By then, my mind would have settled down, too, and I'd be able to see how my mood and not the "unmade bed" was "the issue." So I'd come home from the gym and give him a hug. Both of us would have understood what had happened, and there would be no need to apologize or talk about it. We would be able to move on from it, with no residue.

Now, imagine what would have happened if my partner and I were completely unaware of the role our moods play in our lives and our relationship! All those thoughts I had about the unmade bed would appear to me not as thoughts but as real issues that needed to be addressed one way or another. I would be convinced, in those moments, that we have a problem in our relationship. This is why it is incredibly helpful when two people can see that so many problems and issues are not real; they are mostly "made up" when we're in a low mood.

When it comes to our relationships, we could replace "the bed" with anything else we have expectations about. I had a lot of expectations about how the bed should be made. When my expectations were not met, and I was in a low mood that day, I'd end up having a lot of thoughts about my partner. For a long time, I did not realize that, when in a good mood, I wouldn't care at all about whether he made our bed, or how he made it. It wouldn't be a big deal.

We all have a lot of expectations about all kinds of things. We have a lot of thoughts going on about how and when anything should be done. We have expectations about how our partners should behave or react, and about what they should know by now. We have expectations about how they should feel or how they shouldn't feel about anything.

And we have a lot of expectations about how our relationships should work. When in a good mood, it appears as though we don't have any expectations and, even if we do and they're unmet by our partners, we don't make a big deal out of it. But, when in a bad mood, we're not only aware of all our expectations, but we also are aware of our partners failing to fulfill them. Now we have an issue or issues. We are pissed off.

We have a lot of thoughts around expectations. In particular, when we compare ourselves to other couples, or when we read an article where a relationship expert tells us what our relationship should be like, how often we should have sex, how we should talk to each other, and so forth.

We don't realize how other couples live has nothing to with us. What the relationship experts say may or may not be right, but we forget what they say is just their point of view, not the ultimate truth or the ultimate key to a happy relationship.

More often than not, we don't even realize that our expectations become the lenses through which we view our partners and our relationship. Because of that, we cannot see what is there; we can only see what isn't there, or what's lacking according to our expectations. As soon as they are not met, we feel disappointed. Then we make up all kinds of stories about what it means about our partners and, of course, about our relationship. That's how we end up feeling insecure, unhappy, angry, or sad.

It has nothing to do with what is actually happening, or with our partners. It has nothing to do with the "bed" that he did not make properly again. It has everything to do with our expectations and the meaning we attach to them. And, when we are in a low mood, we attach a lot of meaning to our expectations.

Does it mean it is best not to have any expectations? No. I'm not saying that. We will always have some expectations. We're human, remember? What matters is that we are not so rigid about them. What matters is that we give each other the freedom to screw up sometimes. And remember that it can only be a big deal if we make it so. And that it has more to do with our moods on any given day, then with the fact that he or she screwed something up.

When we are able to see how much of what goes on in our relationships is down to our moods, it really helps us to be more relaxed about the "issues," and the dramas that are a normal part of every relationship. It allows us to embrace each other's humanness. There's a sense of freedom that comes with that. We are able to give each other the space to be ourselves. In that space, there's plenty of room for all that is happening in our relationships, for the "good" and for the "bad'.

In that space, it is OK to screw up sometimes. There's room for our arguments and our meltdowns. And, because there's room for all that, we are able to see that our relationships are good, when good things happen, and they are still good when what happens is not so good. But what makes a big difference ultimately is that we no longer hold each other responsible for how we feel. Instead, we give each other the freedom to feel whatever we feel at any given moment. And that's what gives our relationships the potential for the "happily ever after."

OK. But let's talk about other people. Why? Because we kinda have to deal with people on a daily basis. And when we put ourselves out there, in a big way or in a small way, people will talk about us. People will make comments. They will be making positive comments, and they will be making negative comments, too. We'll also come across a certain type of people, mainly on the Internet. They are called *trolls* or *haters*. So, if you want to make sure your life doesn't suck, it's important that you know how to deal with these people and anyone else who criticizes or disagrees with us.

7

WHAT PEOPLE SAY OR THINK HAS NOTHING TO DO WITH YOU.

Nobody can make you feel anything.

People don't have this much power.

Before I came across the *inside-out* understanding, I used to take what people said or wrote personally, more often than not. At the time, you'd hear me say that their words "made" me feel one way or another. It wasn't a belief. I genuinely experienced it that way, and I think it is fair to say that most people experience it that way too. We don't do it on purpose. It's innocent. Until we realize that there's a different perspective, and we are willing to consider it. My own perspective had changed the moment I realized that how I feel about anything anyone says or writes, has everything to do with my thoughts about it.

By now, you know that we are mostly unaware that we think all the time. We don't need to. How we feel at any moment is our clue. Whatever we feel is a reflection of our thoughts. And we have a lot of thoughts about what other people say or write. When in a low mood, we tend to take words very personally because we attach a lot of meaning to those words. When in a good mood, we don't take what's said or written personally. Instead of being reactive, we become more discerning. We choose whether we want to respond to someone, how we want to respond or whether we want to respond at all to whatever someone said or wrote.

Let me tell you. Whenever I feel angry, stressed, insecure, or sad, I am very reactive. In those moments, it appears as though someone's words have triggered my reaction. I attach a lot of importance to what someone says to me in person, or to what someone writes in their comments on social media. Sometimes, their words don't have to be addressed to me. They may be directed to a person I follow and like. It doesn't matter. When in a low mood, I will react to those words.

Recently, I have been thinking a lot about what people will say about my book! And, I have been freaking out about negative comments. Even though my book hasn't been published yet and, so far, nobody has said anything about it. Either way, when in a low mood, I am very sensitive to what other people say, whether they are complete strangers, my family, or friends. If I don't like what I hear, I can be very reactive. And, you can be sure that on days like these, when you listen to me say: *I don't give a shit* about what someone said - I actually do give a shit! Big time!

And yet, when my mind is quiet, I feel calm. My mood is good, too. And, when I'm in a good mood, how I feel about what anyone says or writes is very, very different. Often, the words that pissed me off or hurt me only a few days ago, now appear to me as nothing but words. I don't get upset or outraged just because someone expressed an opinion that's very different from mine. I simply recognize the fact that if I want to feel free to express my opinion and to feel one way or another about something, then other people have the same right. Rather than being reactive to negative feedback, I actually pause and see if I can learn from it. If someone doesn't like what I said or wrote, I simply respect their right not to like it. I am less reactive and more discerning. I am able to choose conversations that are truly worth being part of and ignore those that are not. And, when someone is unkind or says unpleasant words, I can easily get past it. I don't have to try. I just do.

The *inside-out* understanding allows us to see that nobody can "make" us feel anything, even though it appears to be the case. Instead, we are aware that how we feel about anything anyone says or writes has everything to do with how we feel in those moments. This awareness alone is a real game-changer. It allows us to have a healthy distance to what anyone says, which means we are less sensitive and reactive, and there's a whole lot of well-being that comes from that.

And yet, a lot of advice on how to deal with negative comments, or with *trolls* and *haters* is based on the premise that someone can "make" us feel something. Some suggest that we should not take what people say personally. I don't know about you, but when I am already pissed off or hurt by what someone said or wrote, trying not to take it personally isn't easy! In fact, it rarely works.

. . .

Others suggest that we should only care about the opinions of those who really know us and whose opinions we value. And yet, there have been many instances when the people who know me and who I care about expressed their opinion or shared with me their feedback but, if I were in a bad mood, I'd still take what they said personally. I'd again feel upset or angry if I didn't like what they said, and it wouldn't matter in those moments that I generally care about their opinion or about their feedback.

Which is why the moment we can truly see that nobody can "make" us feel anything, how we perceive what anyone says or writes changes. We become less focused on what's said and more aware of how we're feeling the moment we hear or read anything. We don't blame anyone for how we feel. We don't attach so much importance to words. We no longer need to know how to stop worrying about what someone said. Instead, we grant ourselves the freedom to worry sometimes, to react, and to take things personally because we're human.

Deep down, we know that it is never what people say or write that rocks our boats (even though it sure feels that way when we're in a low mood). The moment we truly get that, our relationships with people become lighter. We don't attach as much importance or meaning to whatever anyone says. We give ourselves and others the freedom to express themselves, even when we might not like what they say. We become better listeners. We don't have the need to impose our views on others. We are more curious and more open. We don't get sucked into meaningless exchanges. Instead, we have more meaningful conversations.

. . .

But let's talk some more about the so-called trolls, haters, and people who say or do horrible things. And, I would like to start with this quote, by Tim Kreider:

> *"One of the reasons why we rush so quickly to the vulgar satisfaction of judgment and love to revel in our righteous outrage is that it separates us from the impotent pain of empathy, and the harder and messier work of understanding."*

You have probably noticed that the word "outrage" is a big word these days! I have seen this word used to describe people's reactions to a humanitarian crisis, and I have seen the same word used to describe people's reactions to the news that KFC had run out of chicken! I am not kidding or exaggerating. The word is being used so often that, sometimes, I get a feeling that some people are in a chronic state of outrage every single day. And when people are outraged, there's always a villain.

Sometimes, that villain is someone who says something nasty. Sometimes it can be someone who simply expressed a different opinion, or whose perspective on life, politics, religion, or any subject is radically different from ours. When we don't grant others the freedom to have their own opinions, and we rigidly stick to ours, there's no room for understanding, and there's no room for a real conversation. We don't pause for a moment, take a breath and think whether a) we want to respond to it, or b) how we'd like to respond to it. We don't pause and try to understand their point of view. Instead, all we focus on are their words, and we react to those words.

. . .

I believe the world would suck much less if we were willing to pause, to think, and to understand. If we were willing to separate the words from the person who says them. I'm not suggesting that nasty behaviour, cruel acts, horrible words are OK and that we should tolerate them. I am saying that there's always a context and nuance. When people look at life from the outside-in perspective, their stories, their beliefs feel very real to them, and, in their minds, they justify what they do or say.

The *inside-out* perspective allows us to see people beyond their words, their stories, and their actions. At the very least, we become more understanding. At the very best, we are capable of feeling compassion toward those who say or do horrible things. Being compassionate doesn't mean that we accept, tolerate, or endorse horrible behaviour.

I believe that we are all capable of being "bad," and we are all capable of doing "bad" things. Generally, I consider myself a good person, and people may think the same about me. And yet, from time to time, I can be a bit of an ass. I may choose not to write what I think about the moron who wrote something on social media, but it doesn't change the fact that, in that moment, I still think that person is a moron. In my mind, the reason why I am outraged by what they said may be noble or honorable, but it doesn't change the fact that I am still an ass. I'm just a noble one at that moment. In fact, if you could hear my thoughts about people or what they say on Twitter or Instagram whenever I'm in a bad mood, you'd probably question whether I'm the good and kind person I generally appear to be!

I may want to tell a person to shut the f*@k up and, trust me; I often feel like saying it. The only difference is that I choose not to. When in a low mood, I may feel I hate someone. I may not write it or say it out loud, but it doesn't change the fact that at that moment, I feel I hate them. Does that make me a better person? Or does it make me a bad person?

The only difference between me and the so-called *trolls* or *haters* is that I am fully aware that how I feel and what I feel like saying has everything to do with me and not with anyone, or with what they say. I know I feel this way because I'm in a low mood. I am angry, anxious, or sad. Or because I attach meaning to what's said or written. I am fully aware that on a "good day" when my mood is good, and I feel well, I would not have those kinds of thoughts.

I'd be lying to you if I told you that I never said anything rude or unkind to anyone. I did. More often than not, the person who was on the receiving end would say: It's OK when I went to apologize for my words. That's because whether it was my mum, a friend, or my partner, they looked at me beyond those words. They knew it was my "mood" speaking and not me. That I was probably angry, anxious, or upset at that moment. When we're willing, we are all capable of seeing people beyond what they do or say. We don't have to label a person as "bad" because they say or do "bad" things. We can separate the two.

I also believe that everyone is born inherently good. And yes, it includes the *trolls* and *haters*, too. Nobody is intrinsically evil and, while there may have been some attempts, scientists have not discovered the evil gene, yet. What I also learned is when people are genuinely at peace with themselves, and when they are truly content, it will not occur to them to say or do something to hurt others deliberately. People generally say and do horrible things when they are not OK - when they are anxious, angry, or scared.

I am fully aware that it is much easier for us to focus on words and on someone's behaviour. It's much easier to judge than to try to understand. It is much easier to react and to condemn straight away. It's much more difficult to try and understand a person or their situation, or to separate the person from their words or their actions. But the world would suck much less if we all at least tried to do more of that.

8

CREATE YOUR OWN DEFINITION OF SUCCESS

Success is whatever YOU make it be.

One of the coolest things about inside-out understanding is that it fundamentally changes the way we perceive life and everything in it. The moment we discover that we live in a THOUGHT-created reality, we realize that all ideas and concepts are born out of THOUGHT. This means they are up for questioning, and we don't have to accept anything as fixed, or as the ultimate truth. Once we know that, we become more curious, more inventive, creative, and we open ourselves up to a whole new way of seeing and being in the world. When it comes to our personal decisions and choices, we are less focused on what's true to others (i.e., people, society, culture) and much more interested in what feels true and right for us.

I wish I had known this much earlier in my life. In particular, when I was in my late teens and in my twenties when I'd spend a lot of time thinking about which University degree I should go for, or what kind of career would be best for me. In hindsight, I can see how my choices were influenced by others, their ideas, their views, and their expectations. Today, I wish I had known that I didn't have to buy into any of that. I could have created my own definition of success, and I could have chosen a path that was aligned with my natural talents and my genuine interests.

Being successful means a great deal to a lot of people. Success is generally associated with money, material possessions, fame, and status. It is a concept that is deeply ingrained in our cultures. There's nothing inherently wrong with it. What so many of us don't realize is that ultimately, it is just that - a concept. It is made up, and we don't have to buy into it. We don't have to treat it as our point of reference when we are making our decisions and choices. And yet, a lot of us innocently do that. We attach a lot of meaning to it, in particular, when we appear to have failed to achieve success. Then, we have a whole lot of thoughts about what it means about us, and more often than not, those are not particularly pleasant thoughts. This is how we end up feeling bad about our lives and ourselves. On top of that, we compare ourselves with those whose lives epitomize success (by its conventional definition) and then have even more unhelpful thoughts about that.

If you want to make sure your life doesn't suck, there are two things I'd like you to bear in mind.

One. When it comes to you and your personal life, you are an expert on you. You are your own personal guru, and your own inner wisdom is the infinite source of guidance available to you 24/7. With so much information out there and so many people (parents, friends, experts, motivational speakers, etc.) sharing with us their views, it is absolutely essential that you don't let your own inner voice, and your intuition drown in the ocean of other people's ideas and concepts about who you should be, what you should be doing and how you should be doing it. By all means, read and listen to others, but always remember to check-in with yourself, to see whether what you read or hear truly resonates and feels right to you.

For whatever reason, whenever we feel stuck or confused, we tend to reach out to others for advice or for guidance. We either talk to someone, listen to some videos or podcasts, or read self-help books. Our attention goes outwards in those moments, as if by default. We're already so caught up in our thoughts about whatever issue it is we're dealing with that, more often than not, more information only adds up to the noise in our heads, and we end up feeling even more overwhelmed and confused.

Whenever you find yourself feeling this way, take a moment and pause. Instead of reaching outwards for guidance, shift your focus inwards. Take some time. Reflect and tune into your own inner wisdom. It isn't difficult. We're simply not used to doing that. Our inner wisdom always wants to guide us, but we cannot hear it when there's a lot of noise in our heads, and we're "drowning" in the ocean of information we never stop to absorb.

Two. Get good at "crap detecting" whenever you read or listen to other people's advice. Be curious. Take some time to reflect on what you hear or read. You don't have to follow anyone's advice blindly, no matter who they are. Too often, when an expert or authority, personal growth coach, or guru share with us their ideas and advice, we turn off our "crap detector." We rely far too much on what they say and forget to check in with ourselves whether the information truly resonates with us.

When we get good at "crap detecting," we develop a healthy distance toward anything anyone says, and we naturally begin to rely more on our intuition. We have the ability to see that ultimately, whatever anyone says is nothing but a reflection of their thoughts, and it is their perspective. It is not the ultimate truth. When we are aware of that, we develop the ability to distinguish information that is truly useful and feels true to us from one that simply isn't.

Success is one of those concepts we rarely look at, question, and reflect on. Instead, more often than not, we blindly follow other people's ideas about what it means to be successful. We read books about it. We listen to podcasts. And, if you are on social media, then you see every day a whole bunch of people who have all kinds of ideas about what being successful means, and what we should do to become successful. There are a lot of so-called motivational speakers who post quotes and videos aimed to motivate us. When our "crap detectors" are off, a lot of those messages can have a huge impact and influence the way we view success and how we view ourselves. Very often we don't realize that what they convey isn't at all helpful.

I would like to show you some examples of the kind of messages I am talking about. I selected a few quotes which I found on Instagram. I was looking for hashtags: "success" and "motivation." While these are only quotes, the messages they convey can often be found in many self-help books or heard during motivational seminars too. When our "crap detectors" are off, when we don't think or question what we read and forget that they only reflect someone's perspective, we can very easily end up being influenced by them.

Let's start with this one:

WINNERS MAKE MONEY

LOSERS MAKE EXCUSES

This quote came with an image. The image contains some guy sitting in (presumably) his own jet. A bunch of $100 bills covers the table he's sitting at. He is wearing a gold chain that looks like it weighs a ton, and a tiger is sitting next to him, for whatever reason. You get the gist.

Where do I even begin? The idea of success, reflected in this particular image, has everything to do with material possessions: the cash, the jet, the golden chain. However, I'm not sure what the poor tiger is meant to convey. Is this your idea of success?

This would be the first question to ask. But the language used in this particular quote is even more important. You can be one or the other, a "loser" or a "winner." There's nothing in between.

Do you feel motivated or inspired when you hear these kinds of statements? That's another question I'd ask myself.

While I find the image rather funny, and I don't even treat it seriously, there are people who use these types of messages and images to motivate others or themselves. They reflect their beliefs about what success looks like and how it is achieved. And not only on Facebook or on Instagram, but in real life too.

I witnessed it myself when I was in Africa last year. Everywhere I looked—on TV, in adverts, in some music videos, and on the streets—there were plenty of private jets, big furs, cash, fancy cars, and hot chicks. And all of this takes place in a country where so many can barely make it through the day because they have nothing, or very little, anyway.

The "winners" and "losers" categories appear to be very popular on Instagram. Let's take another one:

WINNERS ARE NOT PEOPLE WHO NEVER FAIL.

BUT PEOPLE WHO NEVER QUIT.

At first glance, it kind of makes sense. Because it's true that everyone fails, and failure is a normal part of the process when we're trying to achieve our goals. So it's good news that it's OK to fail. And you're still a winner, even when you fail. Let's not forget about that.

. . .

But wait. There's a catch. You can only be a winner if you never quit. Shit! I'm a loser then, given that I quit many things many times in my life. Can you see how much nonsense two simple sentences can contain? Remember, this is a quote that is meant to inspire you and to motivate you.

Here's another one.

IF YOU DON'T HAVE

REALLY BIG DREAMS AND GOALS,

YOU WILL END UP

WORKING FOR SOMEONE ELSE.

It sounds almost like a "threat" to me! I thought that it would be great to work for someone like Richard Branson?! Silly me. The message here is this: make sure that you have not just big dreams and goals, but REALLY big dreams and goals, OK? Because you're clearly screwed if you don't.

Kidding aside, it doesn't matter whether your goals and dreams are small, medium, or big. What matters is that they are YOURS and that you do whatever the hell you want to do! In reality, it doesn't matter if you work for someone else or for yourself. What matters is that you chose the options you are naturally drawn to. What matters is that you like what you do. Full stop.

OK. Last one.

. . .

GOOD THINGS COME

TO THOSE WHO SWEAT!

I'm sure it is true if we're talking about working out in the gym and trying to develop that six-pack, damn it! But sarcasm aside, there are many quotes and many variations on the same theme, which is that in order to achieve goals and dreams we need to work really hard for it. And, of course, sweat a lot while we're at it. I can see how it makes sense to many people.

Since success is always associated with hard work, I would like to show you that the concept of "working hard" means different things to different people. When we buy into the idea that working hard means nothing but sweat and tears, we innocently do not even consider a different possibility.

Ever since I came across the inside-out understanding, I saw very clearly that working hard has very little to do with the number of hours, days, or months we need to spend working toward something. Instead, it has more to do with how we feel about work. How we feel about work has everything to do with our thoughts about it.

This is why you can have a bunch of people who work hard but feel demotivated, stressed, and exhausted, mentally, and physically, who wish they could be doing something else. And you can have a bunch of people who work hard, but who feel exhilarated, totally motivated, who may be physically exhausted on the outside, but who feel very much alive on the inside. And it can happen even when both groups are doing the exact same job.

If you have ever worked on something you were passionate about or on something you truly loved, then you know exactly what I am talking about. You may be able to recall how you felt. Time either flew by really fast, or it felt like it didn't even exist. You were so immersed in what you were doing that you may have forgotten to eat or sleep!

You were able to spend hours and days on whatever you were working on, and you may have been exhausted, but at the same time, you felt alive. It's as if you had this internal engine driving you from within. No obstacle would ever be a problem because you knew you'd find a way to deal with many challenges along the way. You worked hard, but it didn't feel hard! It felt fun! It felt exciting!

But what if you have never experienced anything like that? Does it mean that whatever work you get to do will always feel hard? What if you haven't had a chance to do the work you are passionate about because you haven't found it yet?

If that's the case, don't despair. Contrary to what's commonly believed, just because someone may have found that "thing" they love, it does not mean they never get discouraged, that they never procrastinate, that they never doubt themselves, or that work feels like smooth sailing to them 24/7! That's a major misunderstanding.

There are people who do jobs most of us would never want, jobs we consider menial and boring, and yet they find their work fulfilling. How is it possible? How we experience work on any given day is generated from within. It has everything to do with our thoughts. How we feel about work is a reflection of our thoughts. And, how we feel about it is reflected in the attitude we bring to work.

The bottom line is this. When we can truly see that we live in a THOUGHT-created reality, we realize that all ideas and concepts are up for questioning. When we forget that, we often end up treating ideas, theories, beliefs, and concepts as ultimate truths. We then allow them to influence how we view ourselves, how we view life and everything in it. What matters is that we are aware of that.

In this chapter, I chose to focus on our (and other people's) thoughts about success. When we chase someone else's ideas about success, we are moving further away from what's true to us and from our true desires. When you take time to reflect on your own thoughts about success (and anything else), you will discover a lot about yourself. Life really sucks less when rely on self-knowledge more and less on what other people suggest we should be or do, and when we realize that it doesn't matter what success means to other people. What matters is what success means to us and that we get to define it for ourselves.

DO MORE OF WHAT YOU WANT AND LESS OF WHAT YOU THINK YOU SHOULD. AS OFTEN AS POSSIBLE.

Should remove body hair should not remove body hair.

Should be further away on this project.

Should not want to leave home while my kids are still awake.

Should feel more comfortable in this circumstance.

Should be over that thing, I was grieving.

Leandra McCohen

I think most of us would agree that we have free will. We get to choose what we want to do. Yet so many of us choose to do, not what we want, but what we think we should do. We make plans. We get started. We commit. We work hard. Often, we're struggling, and we're wondering why. What we do feels like hard work or an uphill ride.

But we don't stop. Because one should never give up! Oh no! So, we keep on going. We may end up achieving all the things we set out to achieve. We may feel proud. We may have a sense of satisfaction, but no sense of fulfillment. We cannot shake off that feeling that something is missing.

If you want to make sure your life doesn't suck, it is essential that you pay attention to your desires and where they come from. That you know the difference between your *wants* and your *shoulds*, and then, as often as possible, you choose to do more of what you truly want and what feels right, and less of what you think you should.

I believe that we're often not aware that we do a lot of what we think we should do, as opposed to doing what we truly want to. Not just in life in general (i.e., a career, a degree) but in our day-to-day lives. Mainly because we rarely pause and examine where our desires come from. We never stop and ask ourselves, other than superficially, what is it that we truly want. There's something else we do. Sometimes we think we want something, but this kind of wanting is just another version of should. Let me give you some examples so you can see what I mean.

We see all the images of fit and gorgeous people every day, in magazines, or on Instagram. We see them going to the gym a lot, and we watch the videos with the exercises they do. Now, we want thaaaat! We want to look like them. We know that to look like that, we need to eat healthily, and we need to go to the gym. So we give it a go.

But, sooner or later, we feel resistance. We don't feel like

How To Make Sure Your Life Doesn't Suck

running on the treadmill or eating goji berries for breakfast. So we stop going to the gym. And we stop eating the goji berries. Now we find the same images of the same fit and gorgeous people upsetting because when we look in the mirror, all we can see is that we don't look like them. And we probably never will. Now we're asking ourselves, what's wrong with us? Why can't we be like them? Why can't we get up every day to go to the gym at 6 am? Why can't we enjoy the damn goji berries for breakfast?

Or.

Remember our friend Joe from the office? He is now a successful entrepreneur. He owns his own business. We know that because we follow him on Facebook. He works when he wants and wherever he wants. He often posts pictures of himself with his laptop working on a sunny beach.

This time he is in the Maldives. He looks great. He looks happy. Oh, and he is sipping on a strawberry mojito. The caption says: "Another great day in the office." The office, of course, is a stunning villa on stilts, in the middle of the ocean. We, on the other hand, are staring at Facebook, in an office or cubicle because we work for someone else. We don't want to work for someone else anymore, especially when we see our friend Joe. We want what Joe has.

So we quit the job. We now have a business. We used to work from 9-5 pm. Now, we feel we work 24/7. There is so much to do and think about that; sometimes, we forget to eat or take a shower. And we just received a postcard from the Maldives. Joe sent it because Joe loves to send postcards.

It says: "Good luck with your business. How exciting!." But we're not grateful for his kind words. We're pissed off. We're jealous. We begin to question our abilities. We have lots of doubts. We don't feel excited or motivated. But we are definitely exhausted, physically, and mentally. And we look back at when we did the 9-5. Now it feels like a luxury, and we miss our cubicle and our office.

When we compare ourselves to others, at some point, we may end up thinking that what they do sounds like a good idea or sounds like something we'd want to do. That what they have looks like something we might want to have, too. If we never pause and reflect, we may end up doing things we never truly wanted.

It only takes a bit of awareness and some willingness to pause and reflect from time to time to see the difference between a true desire and one that's made up. Then it takes a bit of awareness about what we are actually comparing ourselves to—the carefully selected "best bits" of someone else's life, to their best looks, and to their best or happiest moments. What we don't compare ourselves to is the rest—the fears, the struggles, the tears—the unfiltered humanness we all have in common. The humanness that apparently doesn't look good on Instagram or on Facebook.

I gave you only two examples of how we end up with a bunch of

How To Make Sure Your Life Doesn't Suck

fake *wants* or *shoulds* when we compare ourselves to other people. But I encourage you to find your own examples. Find examples in your own life when you did something you truly wanted and when you did something you thought you should. See the difference and feel the difference between the two.

There is another way we end up with a bunch of *shoulds*. I would like to talk a bit more about the "how-to books" and anyone else's advice.

These days we have thousands of the "how-to" books. We can find a ton of information written by experts who tell us how to manage time, how to write a book, how to be successful, how to overcome fear or resistance, how to be more aware or more spiritual, and so forth.

You know, by now, that I am not trying to discourage you from reading these books. I read a lot myself, and I love to be well-informed. What I have found is that many people (including myself), for a reason I don't quite understand, rely far too much on what the experts and gurus say. It seems that, as soon as "an expert," "scientist," or a "guru" writes a book on any subject we might be interested in, we stop listening to our own wisdom, and we end up treating what they say as the ultimate truth.

I would like to show you how it plays out and what it feels like when we follow anyone else's advice and ignore our own inner wisdom. It's a little story about how this book came into being.

. . .

I have known for a really long time that I wanted to write this book. I had some ideas about what I would like to write about, but I wasn't 100% sure. I knew with time I'd have more clarity. And, eventually, I did. But even though I was pretty clear about what I wanted to say in the book, I struggled to begin to write it. I could not understand why it was happening. Why couldn't I sit and simply write? What the hell was going on?

So I decided I should probably reach out for some advice from those who wrote and published their books already. I read books, blogs, and articles on "how to write a book." Of course, there were tons of ideas and tips shared by different people and experts in this area.

I finally chose the advice which sounded most appealing to me. It sounded exciting and straightforward because the person who shared it claimed it was possible to write a book in twenty or thirty days. It sounded like a great idea, indeed. I learned that all I had to do was to sit down every day and write and do it every day for a period of time. No exceptions. I liked this part too because I also thought that I should have a discipline of some sort. It was also suggested that I should have the same spot where I would work and, preferably, sit down to write at the same time every day. So now, I had a plan, and I was eager to start.

But I struggled on day one, and then I struggled on day two. Then I struggled on day three until I had enough of trying to follow the advice and do what is asked of me. I stopped trying. In fact, I was tired of reading another blog or a book in search of a different or a better idea. In the meantime, I started to doubt myself.

All I thought about was why I could not write the damned book. I was feeling really low. You may remember me saying, earlier in the book, that when we feel low and begin to wonder why we do, we'll end up finding all kinds of "reasons." And they will all sound really compelling to us. The reason I came up with was I wasn't a writer, and I couldn't write. And I must have been crazy to think that I could in the first place. Maybe I should go and learn to write, or maybe I should simply give up.

Eventually, I decided to just get on with my life and forget about the book. A week later, I sat down in front of my laptop to do something else with no plan to write, but I started to write. I did not stop for a week, except when I slept or had something to eat. This is how I ended up with the first draft.

In between then and now, when I am working on my last draft, I had quite a few meltdowns and moments when I could not write. But by then, I knew better. I did not reach out for any book or any advice in those moments. Instead, I listened to my own inner wisdom. I accepted the fact that I was stuck, so I let go of trying to write and shifted my focus onto something else. And, of course, soon, I was back on track and writing again.

If I listened to the expert opinion on how to overcome resistance, which I felt countless times in the process, I'd be pushing myself to write, no matter what. I did that once or twice, but what I produced was crap. Instead, it occurred to me one day; every time

I felt resistance, it was precisely the time to step away from my laptop and go do something else and not think about the book.

This entire book was written when I was not in front of my laptop waging the battle with "resistance" and pushing myself to write. At some point when I went to do something else, eventually, an idea would pop in my head, or a sentence, or a whole paragraph. Just enough to get back to writing. All I ended up doing, once back in front of my laptop, was typing what occurred to me when I wasn't pushing myself to write.

Today, I know that neither "resistance" or "writer's" block" are things we should overcome or treat as a problem. Hugh McLeod, whose book on creativity I love, once said: *"writer's block is just a symptom of feeling like you have nothing to say, combined with the rather weird idea that you should feel the need to say something."*

Resistance is similar. It shows up as a feeling when we can't seem to start a project, but we think we should. It shows up every time we are detached from our own wisdom and rely instead on what others say we should do and how and when we should do it. This includes the *shoulds* we invent ourselves. It shows up when we follow the *shoulds* instead of our true *wants*.

When it comes to all the "how-to" books and any kind of advice coming from anyone else, the point here is to remember that you have your own unique groove, and you have the wisdom to find that groove within you, to find what works for you.

. . .

I'm not suggesting that anyone else's advice is good or bad, right or wrong. What matters is that you use your own inner wisdom to discern which advice (method, tool, strategy) is truly helpful to you at any given moment, and which one is not, or whether you need a method or any tool at all. What matters is that you don't lose your own groove whenever you decide to follow someone else's advice. That you don't let it drown in the ocean of the *shoulds*, you made up in your own head or the *shoulds* that came from anyone else.

The bottom line is when we really want something, we will go and get it. We will go to the gym, and we will eat goji berries. We will write that book. We will run our business from our laptop, somewhere in the Maldives, and drink mojitos while we're looking at our spreadsheets.

When we truly want something, we usually act immediately. We feel inspired. We feel excited. We have this feeling of quiet conviction. We have a hunch or a hint to begin something. We might not know all the steps and all that it will take to get where we want to be. But we sure as hell take the first step. And then another. And another. We don't even have to figure out what the next step is going to be because every step reveals itself as we keep on moving.

We work hard, but we feel at ease with it. We make the effort, but it feels effortless. Every once in awhile, we hit bumps along the way. But it isn't a problem. We're driven from within, and that gives us the confidence and strength to deal with all the bumps and all the challenges we encounter.

. . .

We don't always feel courageous or motivated, but that's not a big deal either. We know sometimes we will feel motivated, and sometimes we won't. Sometimes we will feel resistance, and sometimes we won't. When we are aware of it, we are able to navigate those moments with much more ease. We know, sooner or later, the courage and confidence will naturally re-emerge. So we keep on going. Or it may occur to us that we'd like to chill; have a cup of coffee and do nothing for a bit—however long that "bit" may be. And it isn't a big deal.

We feel very different when we do what we think we should do, or we think we want, but deep down, we really don't. For example, we often find it difficult to take the first step—to begin. We spend a lot of time thinking about all the steps, and all it will take to get us to where we want. Then we feel overwhelmed, even though we haven't started yet. We feel a lot of resistance. And we certainly don't feel motivated or inspired. We begin to wonder if we are good enough if we have what it takes to achieve what we want.

At some point, it may occur to us that it is a lack of motivation that stops us. Or, perhaps, a lack of confidence. So we read self-help books or go to seminars to get confident and get motivated. But at no point do we pause and consider the possibility that maybe that thing we are trying to do or achieve isn't what we truly want; that it might not be our thing. In which case, going to seminars or reading self-help books to get motivated or to become more confident is pointless.

Why would you want more confidence or motivation to do something that you don't really want to do in the first place?

How To Make Sure Your Life Doesn't Suck

What if you're experiencing resistance because your intuition is trying to tell you that thing you're resisting is not your thing?

There is also the possibility the timing isn't right yet. You are not meant to write this book or have that business right this minute. Maybe there are things you still need to learn. But the bottom line is when you truly want something, and when you are truly ready, you will discover that you have all the resources within yourself to make it happen.

Whatever is missing—information, a skill, or money—you know you will figure out what needs to be done to get it. You will find the courage, confidence, and resilience you never thought you had. You will not need to go and get them from somewhere else or generate them by using self-help tools and tricks. They will emerge naturally. It doesn't mean that you will never feel any resistance; you will, but it won't be a big deal. You won't be fighting it. You'll know exactly when to chill and when to keep on going. Whether you feel resistance or not will be irrelevant, and you won't be freaking out about it.

There are, and always will be, things we should do. We might not want to pay our bills, but we know we should! So we pay them. We might not want to go to the dentist, but we know we should. So we go. Even when we do what we love, there will be plenty of things we will not want to do.

We may love the job we do, but we don't like the commute. But we will commute. We may love working for ourselves, but we won't like the admin side of things, but we will deal with it one way or another. When we do what we truly want, none of the day-to-day *shoulds* are a big deal.

When it comes to our life choices, the more we do what we think we should, the less we are in touch with who we are and with our true desires. We often unconsciously end up doing things to fulfill other people's expectations, to fit in, or to please other people. In fact, we may often end up so preoccupied with what others think of us that their opinions and ideas influence a lot of what we do and say. Often, other people's opinions become more important than our own intuitive hunches.

If you want to make sure your life doesn't suck, I highly recommend that every once in a while you pause for a moment, check-in with yourself to see where you're at, see if you're on track, and see if you're following your true wants and less of the *shoulds*. When you hear yourself saying: *I should*, treat it as your clue to ask yourself, at that moment, what you actually want. Deep down, you know what you truly want, even when you think you don't.

The little voice within is always guiding you. It whispers in your ear. It gives you a hunch or a hint. The moment you tell yourself, with full honesty, what you truly want, your mind will settle, and you will naturally find yourself back in your groove.

10

MAKE FRIENDS WITH YOUR FAILURES.

It's really a great asset to be willing to fail and blow it, so to speak,

and to be OK with just making stuff, sharing it, and getting feedback.

Chase Jarvis

Many people know what they truly want. But, what often seems to stand in their way, they'd say, is the fear of failure. It doesn't surprise me at all. From an early age, we have been taught that it is not OK to fail. We learned to see failure as something "bad" or "undesirable," something we should be ashamed of or avoid at all costs. Either way, we learned that failure is a big deal.

In the past, I thought that life would suck less if I didn't fail or if I failed less. Now I know that it isn't the case. Sure, it sucks when we are afraid of failing. But it sucks much less when we realize what we are really afraid of is not failure itself. We are afraid of the thoughts we have about failure. Let me explain.

The fact that we fail has no meaning on its own. Failure on its own is just that, a failure. It's a word that is used to describe when something did not go the way we expected it to have gone. That's all. We can only be afraid of failing when we attach additional meaning to it.

If it is a positive meaning, we will feel OK about it. If it is a negative meaning, we will feel like crap. Some people will say they are afraid of failure because they are afraid of what others will think of them if they fail. Even then, you have to think and speculate beforehand about what people might say in order to feel any fear about it. You are afraid before they had a chance actually to say anything. And we already covered the subject of other people's opinions, remember?

What we think after we failed is how we will end up feeling. We can think all kinds of things. Here are some of them:

I'm a loser.

I won't amount to anything.

I will never be successful.

There is something wrong with me.

What if I never achieve anything I set out to achieve.

I'm worthless.

I am ashamed.

What will people think?

And it goes on and on. It can last for a day or two. It can last for weeks or months and even years. Whatever we think feels true. It feels real. We feel crap. We feel depressed. We feel anxious or stressed. The longer we continue to think this way, the longer those feelings will persist. But whatever we think has nothing to do with the failure and it has nothing to do with who we really are either.

But, as we've already explored, thoughts and our moods change. We wake up. We look at the failure again. It looks different to us now. Now when we are in a better state of mind when our mood is brighter, and our thinking is clearer, we may think:

I'm glad I failed because I realized I actually didn't want to work on that anymore.

If I didn't fail, I just would not have noticed this or that opportunity.

Yes, I failed. But, at least I gave it a go. I'm proud of myself.

I learned a lot because I failed at it.

In a way, I'm glad my relationship failed. Now I know what I truly want when I go into the next one.

Now I know what love means to me.

So what that I failed? What's the big deal? I'm moving on to the next thing with a bunch of lessons I learned about myself.

. . .

And so on, and so forth.

Whatever we think, the bottom line is this: failure alone means absolutely nothing. Sometimes we feel really bad about it. And sometimes we feel OK. We're never really afraid of failure, but we damn sure think scary thoughts, and we freak out because we think these thoughts. It seems to me that there is only one difference between those who succeed more often and those who don't. Those who do, don't treat their failures too seriously because they don't treat their thoughts too seriously, knowingly or not.

11

THE FUTURE DOES NOT EXIST. SO YOU DON'T NEED TO WORRY ABOUT IT.

The future is made of present moments.

Other than being afraid of failure, I used to be afraid of what the future holds. I spent a lot of time thinking about it. More often than not, I'd end up freaking out because the more I hung out with my thoughts about the future, the more depressed or anxious I'd become.

I remember clearly what I thought about the gurus or spiritual teachers who claimed that the future didn't exist. So, when I say the future doesn't exist, please know, I understand you might be surprised or baffled and even think that I've lost it. Please don't throw the book away and let me explain what I mean when I say that it doesn't exist and why our lives would suck less if we understood how and why we end up worrying about it.

. . .

I first heard a similar statement many years ago, and I ignored it. I thought the person who said that was a detached-from-reality lunatic, so I was not going to pay any attention to what they were saying. From my perspective, at that time, the future definitely existed.

My attitude changed when, years later, I experienced the "aha" moment I was telling you about earlier in the book. You may remember me saying that nothing had changed when it happened, but everything looked different to me. What also changed for me was that I replaced my dismissive attitude with curiosity. I realized that day that nothing is as it seems. Everything is up for questioning. And just because someone says something that makes no sense to me right away, does not mean there's no truth or sense in it. And it is generally a good idea to try to understand what's said first before I dismiss it.

By the way, it is a very human thing to have different beliefs and different points of view. It is a very human thing to argue and to disagree. I still argue, and I still disagree. I can be very stubborn when it comes to defending my views and my beliefs. Ask my friends and family. Just because I experienced the "aha" moment, does not mean that I stopped being human. I'm simply less of a righteous "I know better" kind of person and more of a curious person. And what I found is that it makes life much richer and more interesting.

So I got curious about "the future."

No matter who I teach, coach, or speak to, no matter their age,

How To Make Sure Your Life Doesn't Suck

gender, or social status, "the future" has always played a big part in our conversations. There are two issues that have been common themes.

One. They worry about the future. Some are really scared. Some are terrified.

Two. They don't know what they want to do in their lives, and they are scared that if they don't figure it out and if they don't do it fast, they will be screwed, and so will their future.

Boy, could I relate to all of that!

Imagine what would happen if I told them that there was no future and that they should stop worrying about it! I can imagine all kinds of scenarios, including one, where I would end up with a black eye!

First, I'd like to explain to you why I'm now one of those people who think the future doesn't exist.

The future is not a tangible thing because it can only exist in our thoughts. We can only think about the future. We can speculate about it and even try to predict it. By doing so, we can come up with all kinds of scenarios. But, right now, at this moment, "the future" can only exist in our thoughts! We can never know what the future holds, and we can never be certain about what will happen in the future. Life brings all kinds of twists and turns. We choose different paths. We make choices. All those things will determine where we will end up, eventually.

The only thing that's tangible is what we can do right now, this moment, today. Because after one present moment comes the next. And then another. The future is what's made of all those present moments coming together. Life would suck much less if we could remember that more often! We would spend more time enjoying the moment and getting things done, as opposed to freaking out about what may or may not happen in the future.

Does this mean that we should all just sit, smoke some weed, and listen to Bob Marley? Forget everything and hope for the better? No. That's not what I'm saying.

I am not suggesting that you sit and do nothing or that you don't think about your future! Of course not. What I am suggesting is that there is a huge difference between thinking about the future and worrying about the future. I won't tell you how to stop worrying. I want to explain to you how we end up worrying.

I'm sure there are tricks and methods you can use to stop worrying now. But, sooner or later, you will start to worry again, if not about your future, then about something else. When you understand why and how worrying happens, you will be more relaxed about it if and when it happens. Since you will be more relaxed about it, your life will suck less, too.

How To Make Sure Your Life Doesn't Suck

. . .

We established that we can only think about "the future." And when we think about it, we can come up with multiple scenarios. It only takes these two words: "what if..." and you're on a roll! Your imagination kicks in. You now have the empty canvas in front of you. Remember, your thoughts are the brushes. The painting you end up with is a reflection of your thoughts.

It will either be beautiful, and you'll feel excited or inspired when you look at it. Or it will be ugly, and you'll feel deflated or depressed. But whatever you're looking at is NOT your future. What you're looking at is just a painting made up of your thoughts!

We have the tendency to think about our future, especially when we feel low. For example, you may be worried about the bills that you'll have to pay in a month or two. You begin to think about it. Your imagination kicks in. You see all kinds of terrible scenarios. By now, you can even see yourself as a homeless person because you did not pay your bills. So you feel scared. On top of that, you feel shitty about yourself. You wonder why you're not successful yet and will you ever have the money to do the things you want, or will it always be this way.

Now you feel even worse. And because you feel worse, you feel uninspired. You feel stuck. Because you hang out in the ugly painting of "the future," you are not present anymore. And, because you're not present here and now, you cannot see what could actually be done about your bills! It may not be what you wanted. It may not be an ideal solution. But you'd always come up with one when you stop hanging out in "the future" and start hanging out in the now.

If you're going to think about your future, choose your time wisely. Make sure you are in a good mood when you do so. Make sure you're feeling OK. When you're in a good place, thinking about your future will not only be fun, but it also will be creative and productive. You'll know because you'll feel good, you'll feel inspired, you'll gain clarity as to what needs to be done, and you'll be eager to get going.

When you feel crappy, you'll only end up getting a crappy painting of your future. Don't even "go there." Check-in and see how you feel. If you feel low, that's a signal. It is NOT the time to think about your future. Go for a walk. Watch Netflix. Do something else. Do something you like.

Finally, always remember that whatever you think about the future IS NOT a prediction of your actual future! It is not a preview. It's just a painting. And, whether it is ugly or pretty, it is still just painting and NOT your future.

Before we move away from "the future," I want to talk a little about an issue that is related — the "I don't know what to do in my life" issue. As I said earlier, it is a subject that often comes up in my conversations with many people and, in particular, with young adults. I have been dealing with this issue myself pretty much all my life.

. . .

The idea that you should know what you want to do in your life is a belief. Beliefs are simply a reflection of your (or someone else's) thoughts. They are not facts. The question you might want to ask yourself is one that Seth Godin asks in one of his books:

"Why does it bother you?

No one actually knows what to do.

Sometimes we have a hunch or a good idea, but we're never sure.

It's about doing something when you're not certain it is going to work."

Of course, there are people who have always known that they wanted to be astronauts since kindergarten. You can replace "astronauts" with any profession. And that's great. Sometimes I wish I were one of those people. But what I also wish is that someone had told me that not knowing what I wanted was not a problem! Just because I didn't know what I wanted to do with my life (and I didn't know for a long, long time), I wasn't a failure. Because I didn't know, it did not mean that I wouldn't amount to anything! Had I known this much earlier in my life, my life would definitely suck less.

So I am telling you this now. You don't need to know what you want to do with your life. Life isn't linear. You will be evolving as a person throughout your life. What matters to you now might not matter to you later on. What sounds like a great career choice right now may not sound great anymore in a few years. Your priorities, your preferences, your likes, and your dislikes will be changing, too. Life will bring all kinds of situations that will impact the course of your life and your choices.

You may be worried whether the choices and decisions you make are right or wrong. But you cannot know that. The very reason why we struggle to make certain decisions is that we think about the outcome too much, and we think we can predict it with certainty! The brushes are out, and we turn into artists. Now we're painting all kinds of paintings of what the outcome might be.

But it is only what we think it might be. It is only what we are imagining. And we either freak out, or we feel inspired by the possibility. There is no outcome. The "unknown" that many of us are afraid of is just a word. It is what we imagine in the picture of the "unknown" and what we paint in it that will make us feel one way or the other about it.

While we've been playing with the brushes and painting all kinds of scenarios, we forget one crucial detail: we have within us the resilience and resourcefulness to deal with whatever outcome our decisions may bring. We always have. It won't be different next time it happens. So, if you insist on playing the Frida or the Picasso when thinking about the outcomes of your decisions and choices, make sure you keep the prettiest painting. You might as well. After all, it's just a painting.

There's something else. You may not know what you want to do with your life at the moment. But you are still doing something. You never do nothing! Even if you don't work, you are still

How To Make Sure Your Life Doesn't Suck

doing something. Life moves on. You may feel stuck, but unless your legs are stuck in concrete, you're never really stuck. You can only feel stuck. And you feel stuck because you're caught up in your thoughts.

That's a huge difference. You may be doing something you don't like. You may be studying for a degree for the sake of it. You may be doing a particular job just because you have to eat. Your choices and what you do may not make much sense at this very moment. That's OK.

At some point in the future, when we look back at what we did and at our choices, a mysterious thread appears. It connects all our past choices and situations, and there's a logic to it. What did not make sense at the time, now makes perfect sense to us. Even the "tough times" or "bad relationships" we had now look very different to us. What appeared to be a "bad" choice or what seemed to be pointless now makes total sense. There is a thread because the dots somehow always connect when we look back.

When we don't know what to do with our lives, and we think it is a problem, that's when we begin to feel anxious or scared. We feel this way not because we don't know what we want, but because we think we should know! We go into our heads, where we find even more negative thoughts about our lives and ourselves.

Now we do the very same thing we did when we thought about "the future." The thoughts turn into brushes, and we come up with all kinds of paintings. They will be ugly, and we'll feel accordingly. By now, we're so preoccupied with what we see or can't see that we cannot see anything else. With so much noise in our heads, there is no way we can hear the answers to the questions we are asking about our life or our future. There is no way we can hear the little voice within trying to guide us about what we could actually do—perhaps not for the rest of our lives, but what we could do right here and right now.

If you want to make sure your life doesn't suck, all you need to focus on and care about is what can be done right now. What can be done where you are today and with what you have. You know what you love, whatever it is, do more of that, right now. If you don't know what you love, do what makes sense. It's enough.

It might sound lame because we want to know where we will end up. We want to know whether we'll fail or succeed. But we can't know with complete certainty the results of our choices beforehand.

All we need to do is to take the first step. And the first step will reveal another, and then another. If you want to go off into the future, do so when you feel good. Do so because you want to play with ideas, do some blue-sky thinking, and to dream the dream. Don't think about your future when you feel low because you'll end up playing with scary images that you created with your own thoughts, and you'll be freaking out for no reason.

12

DON'T WAIT FOR THE WORLD TO CHANGE.

There is no how-to guide for how to change the world. But it's easy to get hung up by misconceptions about what it takes to make an impact.

Wendy Kopp

There's a lot happening in the world today. Whenever I watch the news, I cannot believe we are still dealing with so many problems that, in my mind, should have been solved a long time ago. I cannot believe that there is still hunger in the world. I cannot believe that people still kill each other. I cannot believe that there are parts of this world where having clean water is a luxury... in the 21st century.

I cannot believe that families break up, and so many people hate each other because of their different political views. I cannot believe that skin color is still an issue to so many people and that they attach any meaning to it. I cannot believe people hate and kill each other over their religious beliefs. I cannot believe there's so much outrage and hatred and so many divisions everywhere I look.

These are often my thoughts.

When I think those thoughts, sooner or later, I feel pretty depressed. In moments like these, I find it difficult to believe that the world will ever change. All I can see is how much would have to change. It looks so immense to me that the only feeling I am left with is a deep sense of helplessness. I cannot see how my actions could change anything. If I cannot do anything to change the world, I begin to look at those who, I believe, could.

I think about governments and politicians. And I wonder why they are not doing enough or why they are doing all the wrong things. I begin to blame them because, in my mind, they are responsible for resolving all the "bad" that is happening today. All I am focusing on now is my anger or sense of helplessness. Everything that needs to change to make this world a better place isn't up to me. It's up to everyone else.

Until I realized one day that I only feel this way because I think those thoughts. I only feel this way because my thinking revolves around what's wrong with the world. When it happens, I cannot see anything else. I cannot see all the good that is happening in the world today. I cannot see all the people that do good and make a difference. If I did, I'd be able to see what's possible. I probably would feel inspired to do something too. I'd be able to see that while I might not be able to change the world, there's a lot in my own world—and in my own head—that can change.

I now know how I see and experience the world has everything to do with how I think about it and what I am focusing my attention on. I now know my gloomy thoughts will reveal a gloomy world, and I will feel miserable. It is this thinking that stops me from seeing the possibilities and solutions—maybe not to all the world problems but the problems that are happening around me, that are happening in my little world.

Now, I know that my gloomy thoughts about all that's wrong with this world don't make it any better. They don't solve conflicts. And they don't end wars. They do not change what's happening in the world. Neither does my outrage or my anger.

Thankfully, there are people who don't wait around for the world to change, who don't wait for governments and politicians to do something. Their energy goes into their work, so they don't waste it by being outraged or angry about what's happening while they're sitting on their couches. Instead, they think about the solutions and take action; they play their part in making the world a better place. I am really grateful I get to meet people like that. I am grateful, so many people today want to be of service to others, and many young people take it into account when they design their future paths and think of their career choices.

In fact, that is the reason why, during my workshops, I love to hear students talk about how we could make the world a better place. I love watching them come up with ideas and solutions. And I love the fact that they see themselves as change-makers and influencers of good change.

But one day, I noticed that when they do come up with ideas, these ideas are often grand. The problems they want to solve are grand too, for instance, global poverty or hunger. There's nothing wrong with that, per se. It simply is a narrow view of what having an impact means, and I like to show them that there are hundreds of things we can do that can be very small and yet equally impactful. I also encourage them to check where their motivations for wanting to make a change come from. Why having an impact matters to them in the first place.

I encourage them, and I encourage you to think about what having an impact means to you. What can you do right now, with what you already have and where you are, that would have a positive impact? Imagine yourself ten or twenty years from now, and imagine that you had a tremendous impact. Perhaps you found a solution that erased hunger in Africa. However, you would not receive any public recognition for it. There would be no accolades. Most people would not know your name. Would you still care about doing something in your life that has an impact?

I am not suggesting that there's something wrong with accolades, public recognition, or your name being known to a lot of people. I'd be a real hypocrite if I told you I don't care about these things. We all do, to some extent. It is not about whose motivations are noble and whose are not. We may have different motivations, but we all have an ego. There's nothing wrong with that.

I ask these questions because they help us discover whether our desire to have an impact comes from our hearts. When we work on something that's deeply rooted in our hearts, everyone wins. Everyone benefits. It has very little to do with what we get out of it and everything to do with what everyone gets from it. That feeling permeates everything we do and how we show up every day. Having an impact stops being only about grand ideas because we begin to see how much impact we can have right here and right now, how much impact we can have everywhere we go, no matter how big or small it may appear to be.

Think about that feeling you get when someone helps you carry your luggage, and you didn't even ask them for help. Or when someone sees you struggle to find change when you're about to pay for your coffee, and they either give you some change or buy you that coffee. I'm talking about that feeling when someone notices how beautiful you look that day. When someone smiles at you on the train. I am talking about random acts of kindness and that feeling you get when you are on the receiving end or when you are the giver. It's that feeling that connects us all!

If we look at each other beyond what we do and what we have, beyond the jobs we do and the titles we carry, beyond the stuff we buy and the clothes we wear, we are all the same. Don't be fooled by appearances. We never know what hides behind the glamorous clothes, perfect makeup, and beautiful smile, behind the costumes we all wear. Likewise, we don't know what hides behind the dirty clothes and messy hair, and the lack of a smile on someone's face. But we can be certain of this: who's there, inside, is a human being with his or her unique story. It is someone who, at the core, is no different than you and me, no matter how rich or poor they are, no matter how "together" or lost they appear to us.

Rest assured that you can and do have an impact every single day — every time you see the person beyond how they appear. You have an impact every time you help someone with anything. You have an impact when you ask someone if they're OK or if they need help; when you sit with them quietly when they're grieving; when you smile at a stranger on the street; when you notice someone needs a break and you're there for them.

You have an impact every time you see a teensy piece of good in the person; everyone considers a threat or evil; every time you forgive someone who thought they would never be forgiven.

When we perceive having an impact as only something impressive or grand, and we only focus on grand problems and grand solutions, we miss out on all the opportunities that are already there in front of our eyes every day. The random acts of kindness that we may perceive as small have a ripple effect, and because of that, there is nothing small about them.

When we can see each other beyond our appearances, we cannot help but see that we are the same, and we have the same basic human needs. In those moments, when we experience people's kindness, and when we are kind to others, we feel connected to each other.

When we feel that someone needs a hand, when we see that someone is struggling, our hearts take over, not our heads. In those moments, we don't care about this person's political affiliations, social status, religious beliefs, or the color of their skin. All we can see is a human being, no different than you and me.

Once we can see one human being this way, eventually we'll begin to see others the same way, too. We will see people for who they really are because we will not be looking at them through the lenses of political, cultural, social, or religious theories and concepts. We'll be able to see clearly that all those ideas, theories, and concepts were born out of someone's belief about people or the world.

And those beliefs and everything that has ever been created was first created in someone's mind. Because all creation begins with the thought. Every problem we're facing today was created because someone first had to think that it was a problem. Every solution was created because someone thought differently. Someone had a new thought. We will know that to see the world differently, we don't have to change the world. We also don't need to wait for other people to change to see them differently. You and I are the change we want to see in this world. All it takes is one new thought to be able to see that.

13

THE END

When wisdom arises, our inherent power as a being naturally arises as well, and then we begin to view things differently.

We begin to see things based on the truth that we have found inside. Not the truth that is imposed by others on us.

M. Laurie Cantil

It may be the end of this book, but it is not the end of your journey.

Life will continue to be one hell of a ride. No matter what we do and how in control of our lives we think we are, life can suddenly shock us or pleasantly surprise us. Sometimes, it can really screw things up for us. The ride can get tough, but you won't be afraid of that. That's life. Sometimes the road is smooth and fun. Sometimes, it is steady and calm. And sometimes, it can get really bumpy or dark.

. . .

But if you look back at everything that has already happened in your life, both the good and the bad, you will find that in the end things turned out fine, and you turned out fine too, regardless of how many roads you had to take or how difficult it was it get to this point. You will discover you may not have had all the knowledge and all the wisdom you have now, but you were enough and knew enough to navigate through life from the very start—without any gurus, coaches, or self-help books.

Do you know why? Because we are never disconnected from our wisdom. It always guides us whether we are aware of it or not. It shows up as a hunch or a hint, or it speaks to us through our intuition. When you look back at your life, you will be able to see it for yourself. You will be able to see when and what your intuition was telling you to do or not to do. It was there all along trying to guide you, whether you had listened to it or not. And, when you look back at your life, you will be able to discover even more about you. More than you ever could, even if you read all the wise books.

You will be able to see that in moments when you felt you were not courageous, you actually were. When you felt lost, you were actually finding your way or yourself. When you felt like you could not go on anymore, you did go on. When you felt insecure and unsure, you still managed to achieve a lot. In times when a situation felt helpless, somehow you found your way out of it. Or you came up with a solution that helped you change that situation. You will find that the people who you felt hurt you, were there for a reason; that relationships that did not work out taught you something valuable. You were able to forgive and forget, even when you thought you never could. You always had enough resilience to get through a lot that happened to you.

When you look back at your life, you will discover a lot about life itself. When you look at all the choices and the decisions you made, at all your failures and all your success and all the people that you had met along the way, a thread will emerge that connects all those moments. You will find that there is a logic to it. Everything that happened in your life happened for a reason that can only be known to you in hindsight.

That all or most of what happened to you somehow made sense in a way, only you can see and relate to. You will discover that the choices you thought were great or best for you at the time, actually sucked. And the choices or situations you thought were bad at the time, ultimately turned out fine and even became the start of something truly great.

And you will discover something else.

You will discover many moments and situations that happened, seemingly, "out of the blue," and all the strange twists and turns that life laid out in front of you. You will see the people, you now know, you were meant to meet. And it will make perfect sense to you why you met them. You will discover that there was a "perfect timing" for everything that happened, even though at the time, you had different ideas about what, when, and how something should have happened.

. . .

Why will you be able to see that?

Because, while there are parts of life in which we actively participate and parts, we have some control over through our decisions and our choices; there seems to be another part of life. The part in which what is happening in it appears to have nothing to with what we do. The part of life that is hidden and intangible. It cannot be measured or rationally explained; it can only be felt. Every once in awhile, we all get that feeling that there is something else going on in our lives. That something else is going on "behind the scenes", that there's more to life than meets the eye.

You may not have a name for it, but you may be able to recognize that feeling. Some people see it as an intelligence behind life. Others call it the universe, or god. Regardless of the label we attach to it; I believe we all get a feeling for it. How it manifests itself or how we experience it will be unique to each one of us.

I recommend you reflect back on your life from time to time. In particular, when you feel like life is kicking your butt, and you cannot understand what it is happening or why. If you step back, even for a moment, and look back at your life, very soon, you will see that perfect thread appear in front of your eyes.

You will be able to remind yourself that if everything that had happened in your life is part of this thread, then so is everything that is currently happening. Just because you can't see how it all connects and how it all makes sense right at this moment, you'll know that you will get to see that eventually. Because of that, you will feel more at peace about whatever is happening in your life right now.

You will also discover you have always had the resilience and resourcefulness to deal with the ups and downs, even when you thought you had none. Somehow you knew how to navigate through life. I hope you'll remember that, before you reach out to anyone for guidance or before you decide to listen to someone else's advice, or before you reach for another self-help book. I'm not saying that you never should (or shouldn't) do that. I am saying that there's an infinity of awesomeness you can tap into any time you need to, and everything you need to know to make sure your life doesn't suck is already within you.

AFTERWORD

You're only one thought away from changing your life.

Wayne Dyer

It has been an absolute honor sharing this book with you.

Thank you for taking the time to read it.

I really hope you found it helpful. I hope this book has opened your mind to a different way of looking at yourself and your life.

When our thoughts change, our experience of life and everything in it changes. Sometimes it takes one insight, one epiphany, one new thought to see life differently. It can happen in an instant. Nothing around us changes but, all of a sudden, everything looks and feels different, lighter. Sometimes change requires more time. More exploration. More reflection. That's OK. There is no right or wrong timing. Whenever change happens, it is exactly when it is meant to happen.

True, sustainable change requires only three ingredients: willingness/openness to change, an open mind and heart, and patience. When these three are in place, true transformation is inevitable. It may not happen fast, it may not come with bells and whistles. It can happen slowly, gradually and quietly. The more aware you remain, the more you will begin to notice how the way you see and experience life and yourself will begin to change.

I hope that this book can play a small part in this process. Perhaps it can mark the beginning of an amazing journey of self-discovery that's ahead of you. Or, perhaps, it can serve as a gentle nudge on the journey that you have already begun.

The way to move forward begins by looking inwards.

If you'd like to explore the topics presented in this book, explore life, problems and issues we're all grappling with and do it with me; then I would love to invite you to subscribe to my podcast "How To Make Sure Your Life Doesn't Suck With Dr. Maggie G."

Afterword

One of the things that bring me joy is hearing from you. If you enjoyed the book, I would love to know:

- What part or parts of the book resonated with you the most and why?
- Did you have any insights you may wish to share?
- What would you like to share with me?
- Do you have any questions?

Email at **me@drmaggieg.com**

I will be addressing your questions and insights on my Podcast. Please let me know whether you'd be happy to have your name mentioned on the Podcast or if you would rather remain anonymous.

If you really, really enjoyed the book and would like to support it, you can do that in various ways by:

- writing a review on Amazon
- subscribing to my Podcast and rating it as high as you can :-)
- sharing the link to the Amazon page with your friends, family and on social media
- sharing with me your insights and thoughts, your photos with the book and your beautiful faces on my Facebook page or, preferably, on Twitter and add #drmaggieg
- If you're feeling super creative and have some fun ideas on how else we could spread the message about my book, I'd be more than happy to hear from you.

I am part of a thriving community of people who, in my view, represent the best of humankind. It is a place where I share my thoughts, my life, my singing, my jokes with others. Where everyone is incredibly fun, kind, and supportive of one another. My Twitter feed is a judgment-free zone where everyone is welcome to hang out with me. Where there's no room for drama or disrespectful behavior but plenty of space for love and laughter. You are welcome to join me there @maggiegilewicz

If you'd like to be informed about my webinars and workshops, please leave your name and email address on my website at www.drmaggieg.com. I promise you won't be hearing from me too much.

I am really excited and looking forward to connecting with you on social media and on my Podcast. We're all in the same human boat! It is much more fun to ride the waves of life together.

Lots of love,

Maggie

ACKNOWLEDGMENTS

To Steve.

Where do I even begin? I wanted to say that I wouldn't have done it without you. "It" - being this book. The truth is, I probably would, but it would have been so much harder! I cannot thank you enough for believing in me, believing that I could write this book before I believed I could do it. Thank you for the countless hours you spent either reading this book again and again or listening to me reading every single chapter! For your notes, for your feedback, for telling me the truth, even if, at times, my ego did not like it! Thank you for putting up with my meltdowns and tantrums whenever I was struggling. Thank you!

To my friends & family.

I am so grateful for each and every one of you, for every phone call, for every chat (particularly those chats that had nothing to do with my book and took my mind of it), for our gym hangouts, for the travels and visits to my home town, for all the coffees we had and for all the laughs! Writing this book took a while. OK, a really long while! Your presence in this process has been my respite and brought me a lot of joy. Thank you for being in my life.

To Michael.

I cannot even begin to tell you how grateful I am to have had the opportunity to spend so much time with you some years ago. I want to thank you for that precious time. Thank you for teaching me about the inside-out understanding, for hanging in there with me when I was struggling to grasp it, for guiding me so I could finally wake up to who I truly was. Finally, I am grateful for the time you took to read this book, for your feedback and for writing the forward.

www.michaelneill.org

To Bill.

Whenever I think of love and kindness, I think of you. I will never forget when I first met you.

You were a stranger then, and I never experienced so much unconditional love during an encounter with someone I didn't know. And, ever since, you have been teaching me and showing me what unconditional love feels like. I am so grateful for your presence in my life. For the kindness and generosity I received from you when I needed it the most. Thank you, Bill!

www.theboothbyinstitute.org

To Arifa.

Whenever I think about how we met, I smile! I want to thank you for being my guinea pig when I was attempting to coach and explain the inside-out understanding for the very first time! But above all, I want to thank you for your friendship. I am so grateful for the time you took to read the manuscript, for all your thoughts and valuable ideas, but more importantly for being there for me when I really, really needed the support of a friend! I will never forget that.

To Lynn.

Thank you for your generosity and the time you spent working on my first draft. When I look at the final draft and compare it to the very first one, I can only imagine it was not an easy task!

To Peter.

Thank you for this amazing book cover. Thank you for your time and your kindness. Your family business is driven by passion and true care, which is why it was such a pleasure working with you.

https://bespokebookcovers.com/

To students of my course at Imperial College London.

You made me re-discover my passion for teaching. You made me realize how much I want to support young adults and help them design meaningful lives, as well as teach them how to navigate emotional highs and lows. Special thanks to Sophia and Ly. You inspired me to write this book. All of you inspired the title.

To my community on Twitter.

Two months ago, I logged into my Twitter with a plan to shut down my account. I have had it for many years, but I never really used it. Just when I was about to quit, I saw a post by this amazing human being. She asked a question, and I answered it. That's all. She saw me and encouraged me to stay. And I did stay. In a little over a month, I went from 210 followers to over 5000. I am part of a thriving community made of mostly writers and amazing human beings from all kinds of backgrounds. It is a place where I can, and I am being fully myself, where I can share my thoughts, joke a lot, laugh out loud, and where I am embraced as I am fully by those around me.

If you ever told me I'd make incredible connections and friendships on Twitter, I'd be skeptical, to say the least. But I did and I would like to thank A. for introducing me to the #writingcommunity; Mira Jeffreys (@mirajeffreys) for making me feel welcomed when I first joined the community and for making me feel loved every single day (and, of course, for being the inventor of the "Doc"); J.D. Greyson (@jdgreysonwrites), Victoria Adeniji (@grlnamedt) and Mike Bowerbank (@wordsmith66) for being there for me through the toughest time just before Christmas. Your kindness, your humor, and your realness touch my heart every day; David DeWinter (@david_dewinter) thank you for your friendship, for being there for me when I needed it the most; Blake Andrew (@samuraismurf73) for your beingness in my little universe; Dennis Rust (@dennis_n_lyrics) we are so alike it is terrifying! Thank you for being there; Wendy Hewlett (@wendyhewlett) and Madelaine Taylor (@beingmaddie3) for the time you spent creating all the social media/podcast artwork, for your patience and, above all, your friendship; Jon-David (@mafiahairdresser) your review touched my soul in a way I cannot even explain. It was more than just an amazing review. It was a confirmation that what I was trying to convey in my book could truly make a difference to people. I will never forget that. Finally, Victoria J.

Price (@victoria_jprice) you are not just a friend, you are like family to me. I am so grateful you entered my little universe.

If you are on Twitter, please follow these amazing human beings and check out their books, their art and enjoy meeting them.

ABOUT THE AUTHOR

Dr. Maggie Gilewicz, aka Dr. Maggie G., is a Sociologist and a Transformative Coach. She helps people from all walks of life understand and navigate their feelings, and see themselves and their lives in a fundamentally different way by sharing the new understanding of mind often referred to as the "inside-out understanding," or the "three principles."

She is passionate about helping young adults design meaningful and fulfilling lives. Otherwise, she lives in London, loves to travel, and sing songs by Ella Fitzgerald after a couple of glasses of wine.

www.drmaggieg.com

Printed in Poland
by Amazon Fulfillment
Poland Sp. z o.o., Wrocław